PSEE
Study Guide

Complete Canadian Public
Service Entrance Exam Study Guide &
Practice Questions

Complete
Test Preparation Inc.
WWW.TEST-PREPARATION.CA

Copyright 2022 Complete Test Preparation Inc. All Rights Reserved.

No part of this book may be reproduced or transferred in any form or by any means, graphic, electronic, or mechanical, including photocopying, recording, web distribution, taping, or by any information storage retrieval system, without the written permission of the author.

Notice: Complete Test Preparation Inc. makes every reasonable effort to obtain from reliable sources accurate, complete, and timely information about the tests covered in this book. Nevertheless, changes can be made in the tests or the administration of the tests at any time and Complete Test Preparation Inc. makes no representation or warranty, either expressed or implied as to the accuracy, timeliness, or completeness of the information contained in this book. Complete Test Preparation Inc. make no representations or warranties of any kind, express or implied, about the completeness, accuracy, reliability, suitability or availability with respect to the information contained in this document for any purpose. Any reliance you place on such information is therefore strictly at your own risk.

The author(s) shall not be liable for any loss incurred as a consequence of the use and application, directly or indirectly, of any information presented in this work. Sold with the understanding, the author is not engaged in rendering professional services or advice. If advice or expert assistance is required, the services of a competent professional should be sought.

The company, product and service names used in this publication are for identification purposes only. All trademarks and registered trademarks are the property of their respective owners. Complete Test Preparation Inc. is not affiliated with any educational institution.

We strongly recommend that students check with exam providers for up-to-date information regarding test content.

Complete Test Preparation Inc. is not affiliated with the Canada Federal Government, nor the Public Service Commission, who are not involved in the production of, and do not endorse this publication.

ISBN-13: 9781772454536

Version 9 January 2025

ABOUT COMPLETE TEST PREPARATION INC.

Why Us?
The Complete Test Preparation Team has been publishing high quality study materials since 2005, with a catalog of over 145 titles, in English, French and Chinese, as well as ESL curriculum for all levels.

To keep up with the industry changes we update everything all the time!

And the best part?
With every purchase, you're helping people all over the world improve themselves and their education. So thank you in advance for supporting this mission with us! Together, we are truly making a difference in the lives of those often forgotten by the system.

Charities that we support -
https://www.test-preparation.ca/charities-and-non-profits/

You have definitely come to the right place.
If you want to spend your valuable study time where it will help you the most - we've got you covered today and tomorrow.

Published by
Complete Test Preparation Inc.
Victoria BC Canada

Visit us on the web at https://www.test-preparation.ca
Printed in the USA

FEEDBACK

We welcome your feedback. Email us at feedback@test-preparation.ca with your comments and suggestions. We carefully review all suggestions and often incorporate reader suggestions into upcoming versions. As a Print on Demand Publisher, we update our products frequently.

https://www.facebook.com/CompleteTestPreparation/

https://www.youtube.com/user/MrTestPreparation

CONTENTS

6 GETTING STARTED
- How this study guide is organized — 7
- The PSEE Study Plan — 7
- Making a Study Schedule — 10

13 ARITHMETIC REASONING
- Self-Assessment — 16
- Answer Key — 20
- How to Solve Word Problems — 21
- Types of Word Problems — 24

32 LOGIC
- Self-Assessment — 35
- Answer Key — 39
- Logic Tutorial — 41

48 SITUATIONAL JUDGEMENT
- Self-Assessment — 51
- Answer Key — 63

69 SEQUENCES
- Self-Assessment — 72
- Answer Key — 75
- Sequences Tutorial — 76
- Types of Number Sequence Problems — 77
- Strategy for Sequence Questions — 79

79 PRACTICE TEST QUESTIONS SET 1
- Answer Key — 123

143 PRACTICE TEST QUESTIONS SET 2
- Answer Key — 179

191 CONCLUSION

192 ONLINE RESOURCES

Getting Started

CONGRATULATIONS! By deciding to take the Canadian Public Service Entrance Test (PSEE 371), you have taken the first step toward a great future! Of course, there is no point in taking this important examination unless you intend to do your best to earn the highest grade you possibly can. That means getting yourself organized and discovering the best approaches, methods and strategies to master the material. Yes, that will require real effort and dedication, but if you are willing to focus your energy and devote the study time necessary, before you know it you will be opening that letter of acceptance.

We know that taking on a new endeavour can be scary, and it is easy to feel unsure of where to begin. That's where we come in. This study guide is designed to help you improve your test-taking skills, show you a few tricks of the trade and increase both your competency and confidence.

The Canadian Public Service Entrance Exam

Sub Test 1 - Reasoning

    Arithmetic reasoning

    Logical reasoning

    Analytical reasoning

    Number or letter series

Sub Test 2 - Judgement

    Situational Judgement

While we seek to make our guide as comprehensive as possible, note that like all exams, the PSEE might be adjusted at some future point. New material might be added, or content that is no longer relevant or applicable might be removed. It is always a good idea to give the materials you receive when you register to take the PSEE a careful review.

How This Study Guide Is Organized

This study guide is divided into four sections. The first section, self-assessments, which will help you recognize your areas of strength and weaknesses. This will be a boon when it comes to managing your study time most efficiently; there is not much point of focusing on material you have already got firmly under control. Instead, taking the self-assessments will show you where that time could be much better spent. In this area you will begin with a few questions to evaluate quickly your understanding of material that is likely to appear on the PSEE. If you do poorly in certain areas, simply work carefully through those sections in the tutorials and then try the self-assessment again.

The second section, tutorials, offers information in each of the content areas, as well as strategies to help you master that material. The tutorials are not intended to be a complete course, but cover general principles. If you find that you do not understand the tutorials, it is recommended that you seek out additional instruction.

Third, we offer two sets of practice test questions, similar to those on the PSEE Exam.

The PSEE Study Plan

Now that you have made the decision to take the PSEE, it is time to get started. Before you do another thing, you will need to figure out a plan of attack. The very best study tip is to start early! The longer the time period you devote to regular study practice, the more likely you will retain the material and access it quickly. If you thought that 1 x 20 is the same as 2 x 10, guess what? It really is not, when it comes to study time. Reviewing material for just an hour per day over the course of 20 days is far better than studying for two hours a day for only 10 days. The more often you revisit a particular piece of information, the better you will know it. Not only will your grasp and understanding be better, but your ability to reach into your brain and quickly and efficiently pull out the tidbit you need, will be greatly enhanced as well.

The great Chinese scholar and philosopher Confucius believed that true knowledge could be defined as knowing what you know and what you do not know. The first step in preparing for the PSEE Exam is to assess your strengths and weaknesses. You may already have an idea of what you know and what you do not know, but evaluating yourself using our Self- Assessment modules for each of the three areas, Math, English and Reading Comprehension, will clarify the details.

Making a Study Schedule

To make your study time the most productive, you will need to develop a study plan. The purpose of the plan is to organize all the bits of pieces of information in such a way that you will not feel overwhelmed. Rome was not built in a day, and learning everything you will need to know to pass the PSEE Exam is going to take time, too. Arranging the material you need to learn into manageable chunks is the best way to go. Each study session should make you feel as though you have accomplished your goal, or at least are closer, and your goal is simply to learn what you planned to learn during that particular session. Try to organize the content in such a way that each study session builds on previous ones. That way, you will retain the information, be better able to access it, and review the previous bits and pieces at the same time.

Self-assessment

The Best Study Tip! The very best study tip is to start early! The longer you study regularly, the more you will retain and 'learn' the material. Studying for 1 hour per day for 20 days is far better than studying for 2 hours for 10 days.

What don't you know?

The first step is to assess your strengths and weaknesses. You may already have an idea of where your weaknesses are, or you can take our Self-assessment modules for each of the test areas.

EXAM COMPONENT	RATE 1 TO 5
Situational Judgement	
Communication	
Being a Team Player	
Building Relationships	
Organization and Planning	
Focus on Customer	
Analytical and Creative Thinking	
ANALYTIC REASONING	
NUMBER SERIES	
LOGIC	
ARITHMETIC REASONING	

Making a Study Schedule

The key to making a study plan is to divide the material you need to learn into manageable size and learn it, while at the same time reviewing the material that you already know.

Using the table above, any scores of 3 or below, you need to spend time learning, reviewing and practicing this subject area. A score of 4 means you need to review the material, but you don't have to re-learn it. A score of 5 and you are OK with just an occasional review before the exam.

A score of 0 or 1 means you really need to work on this area and should allocate the most time and the highest priority. Some students prefer a 5-day plan and others a 10-day plan. It also depends on how much time until the exam.

Here is an example of a 5-day plan based on an example from the table above:

Situational Judgement: 1 Study 1 hour everyday – review on last day
Analytic Reasoning: 3 Study 1 hour for 2 days then ½ hour a day, then review
Communication: 4 Review every second day
Number Series: 2 Study 1 hour on the first day – then ½ hour everyday
Arithmetic Reasoning: 5 Review for ½ hour every other day
Building Relationships: 5 Review for ½ hour every other day
Organization and Planning: 5 very confident – review a few times.

Using this example, Building Relationships and Organization and Planning are good, and only need occasional review. Analytic Reasoning is also good and needs 'some' review. Organization and Planning need a bit of work, Number Series need a lot of work and Situational Judgement are very weak and need the majority of time. Based on this, here is a sample study plan:

Day	Subject	Time
Monday		
Study	Situational Judgement	1 hour
Study	Number Series	1 hour
	½ **hour break**	
Study	Analytic Reasoning	1 hour
Review	Organization and Planning	½ hour
Tuesday		
Study	Situational Judgement	1 hour
Study	Number Series	½ hour
	½ **hour break**	
Study	Organization and Planning	½ hour
Review	Communication	½ hour
Review	Organization and Planning	½ hour
Wednesday		
Study	Situational Judgement	1 hour
Study	Number Series	½ hour
	½ **hour break**	
Study	Analytic Reasoning	½ hour
Review	Organization and Planning	½ hour
Thursday		
Study	Situational Judgement	½ hour
Study	Number Series	½ hour
Review	Analytic Reasoning	½ hour
	½ **hour break**	
Review	Organization and Planning	½ hour
Review	Communication	½ hour

Friday		
Review	Situational Judgement	½ hour
Review	Number Series	½ hour
Review	Analytic Reasoning	½ hour
	½ hour break	
Review	Communication	½ hour
Review	Organization and Planning	½ hour

ARITHMETIC REASONING

This Section Contains a self-assessment and Arithmetic Reasoning tutorials. The Tutorials are designed to familiarize general principles and the Self-Assessment contains general questions similar to the questions likely to be on the PSEE, but are not intended to be identical to the exam questions and the questions here are for skill practice only. The tutorials are not designed to be a complete course, and it is assumed that students have some familiarity with arithmetic reasoning. If you do not understand parts of the tutorial, or find the tutorial difficult, it is recommended that you seek out additional instruction.

The purpose of the self-assessment is:

- Identify your strengths and weaknesses.

- Develop your personalized study plan (above)

- Get accustomed to the PSEE format

- Extra practice – the self-assessments are almost a full 3rd practice test!

Since this is a Self-assessment, and depending on how confident you are with arithmetic reasoning, timing is optional.

The questions below are not the same as you will find on the PSEE - that would be too easy! And nobody knows what the questions will be and they change all the time. Below are general arithmetic reasoning questions that cover the same areas as the PSEE. So, while the format and exact wording of the questions may differ slightly, and change from year to year, if you can answer the questions below, you will have no problem with the arithmetic reasoning section of the PSEE.

The self-assessment is designed to give you a baseline score in the different areas covered. Here is a brief outline of how your score on the self-assessment relates to your understanding of the material.

75% - 100%	Excellent – you have mastered the content
50 – 75%	Good. You have a working knowledge. Even though you can just pass this section, you may want to review the Tutorials and do some extra practice to see if you can improve your mark.
25% - 50%	Below Average. You do not understand arithmetic reasoning problems. Review the tutorials, and retake this quiz again in a few days, before proceeding to the rest of the practice test questions.
Less than 25%	Poor. You have a very limited understanding of arithmetic reasoning problems. Please review the tutorials, and retake this quiz again in a few days, before proceeding to the rest of the practice test questions.

After taking the Self-Assessment, use the table above to assess your understanding. If you scored low, read through the tutorial.

Self-Assessment Answer Sheet

	A	B	C	D
1	○	○	○	○
2	○	○	○	○
3	○	○	○	○
4	○	○	○	○
5	○	○	○	○
6	○	○	○	○
7	○	○	○	○
8	○	○	○	○
9	○	○	○	○
10	○	○	○	○

1. Consider the following population growth chart.

Country	Population 2000	Population 2005
Japan	122,251,000	128,057,000
China	1,145,195,000	1,341,335,000
United States	253,339,000	310,384,000
Indonesia	184,346,000	239,871,000

What country is growing the fastest?

    a. Japan

    b. China

    c. United States

    d. Indonesia

2. A motorcycle is traveling at 100 km/hr. How far will it travel in 2 minutes?

    a. 1.6

    b. 3.3

    c. 1

    d. 12.5

3. Bill invests $4,000 at 8% compounded yearly. How much will he have in 2 years?

    a. $4320.00

    b. $4665.60

    c. $4640.00

    d. $4800.00

4. A waitress serves 10 tables one evening on her shift from 6 - 12:00 PM. She makes $10.50 per hour plus tips. Her total bills come to $240.60 with an average tip of 12%. How much did she make?

   a. 28.87
   b. $63.00
   c. $91.87
   d. $81.87

5. A man buys an item for $420 and has a balance of $3000.00. How much did he have before?

   a. $2,580
   b. $3,420
   c. $2,420
   d. $342

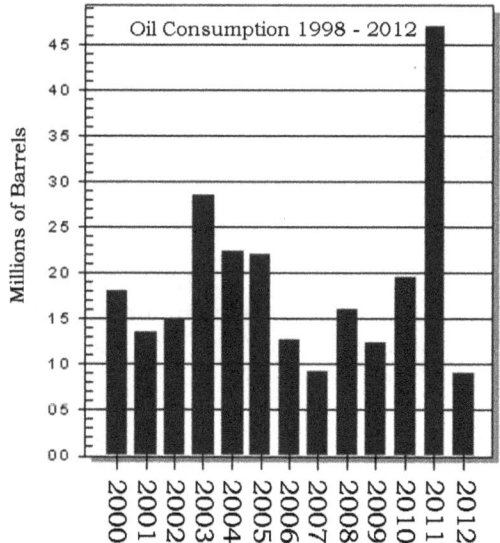

6. The graph above shows oil consumption in millions of barrels for the period, 1998 - 2012. What year did oil consumption peak?

   a. 2011
   b. 2010
   c. 2008
   d. 2009

7. 3 brothers eat a cake in the fridge. Henri eats 1/4 of the cake and Peter eats 2/5. How much is left for Brian?

   a. 7/20
   b. 3/5
   c. 3/4
   d. 9/20

8. A building is 40 feet long, 60 feet high and 20 feet deep. What is the volume?

   a. 40,000 cubic feet
   b. 48,000 square feet
   c. 48,000 cubic feet
   d. 40,000 square feet

9. Susan bought groceries for $29.50 and then met her friend, who repaid her $75 that she borrowed. When Susan got home she had $225.75 in her wallet. How much did she have before?

   a. 150.75
   b. 180.25
   c. 200.75
   d. 201.25

10. A person earns $25,000 per month and pays $9,000 income tax per year. The Government increased income tax by 0.5% per month and his monthly earning was increased $11,000. How much more income tax will he pay per month?

   a. $1260
   b. $1050
   c. $750
   d. $510

Answer Key

1. D
Indonesia is growing the fastest at about 30%.

2. B
First calculate the distance traveled in 1 minute.
100 km/hr. = 100/60 = 1.666 km/minute.
So, in 2 minutes the motorcycle will travel 3.33 kilometers.

3. B
For the first year, $4,000 invested at 8% will be 4000 X .08 = 320. The interest is compounded yearly, so to calculate the second years interest, 4320 X .08 = 345.60.
The total will then be 4320 + 345.60 = $4665.60

4. C
First calculate her hourly wage. 6 hours X 10.50/hour = $63. Next calculate tips. $240.60 X .12 = $28.87. So her total earnings will be 63 + 240.60 = $91.87

5. B
(Amount Spent) $420 + $3000 (Balance) = $3420

6. A
According to the graph, oil consumption peaked in 2011.

7. A
Setup the equation. 1/4 + 2/5 + X = 1
Find common denominator (20) so, 5/20 + 8/20 = 13/20.
So, 13/20 + X = 1.

X = 1 - 13/20
X = 7/20

8. B
The formula for a rectangular solid is Width X Depth X Height - so, 40 X 60 X 20 = 48,000 cubic feet.

9. B
First setup the equation. Let the total before equal X.
(X - 29.50) + 75 = 225.75

X - 29.50 = 225.75 - 75
X - 29.50 = 150.75
X = 150.75 + 29.50
X = 180.25

10. D
The income tax per year is $9,000. So, the income tax per month is 9,000/12 = $750.

This person earns $25,000 per month and pays $750 income tax. We need to find the rate of the income tax:
Tax rate: 750 * 100/25,000 = 3%

The Government increased this rate by 0.5% so it became 3.5%.

The income per month increased $11,000 so it became:
$25,000 + $11,000 = $36,000.

The new monthly income tax is: 36,000•3.5/100 = $1260.

The amount of increase in tax per month is: $1260 - $750 = $510.

How to Solve Word Problems

Do you know what the biggest tip for solving word problems is?

Practice regularly and systematically.

Sounds simple and easy right? Yes it is, and yes it really does work.

Word problems are a way of thinking and require you to translate a real-world problem into mathematical terms.

Some math teachers say that learning how to think mathematically is the main reason for teaching word problems.

So what does that mean?

Studying word problems and math in general requires a logical and mathematical frame of mind. The only way you can get this is by practicing regularly, which means every day.

It is critical that you practice word problems every day for the 5 days before the exam as the absolute minimum.

If you practice and miss a day, you have lost the mathematical frame of mind and the benefit of your previous practice is gone. You must start all over again.

Everything is important.

All the information given in the problem has some purpose. There is no unnecessary information! Word problems are typically around 50 words in 2 or 3 sentences.

Often, the relationships are complicated. To explain everything, every word counts.

Make sure that you use every piece of information.

7 STEPS TO SOLVING WORD PROBLEMS

Step 1 – Read through the problem at least three times. The first reading should be a quick scan, and the next two readings should be done slowly to find answers to these questions:

> What does the problem ask? (Usually located at the end)

Mark all information and underline all important words or phrases.

Step 2 – Draw a picture. Use arrows, circles, lines, whatever works for you. This makes the problem real.

A favorite word problem is something like, 1 train leaves

Station A travelling at 100 km/hr and another train leaves Station B travelling at 60 km/hr. ...

Draw a line, the two stations, and the two trains at either end.

Depending on the question, make a table with a blank portion to show information you don't know.

Step 3 — Assign a single letter to represent each unknown.

You may want to note the unknown that each letter represents so you don't get confused.

Step 4 – Translate the information into an equation.

Remember that the main problem with word problems is that they are not expressed in regular math equations. Your ability to identify correctly the variables and translate the information into an equation determines your ability to solve the problem.

Step 5 – Check the equation to see if it looks like regular equations that you are used to seeing and whether it looks sensible.

Does the equation appear to represent the information in the question? Take note that you may need to rewrite some formulas needed to solve the word problem equation.

Step 6 – Use algebra rules to solve the equation.

Simplify each side of the equation by removing parentheses and combining like terms.

Use addition or subtraction to isolate the variable term on one side of the equation. If a number crosses to the other side of the equation, the sign changes to the opposite -- for example positive to negative.

Use multiplication or division to solve for the variable. What you to once side of the equation you must do for the other.

Where there are multiple unknowns you will need to use elimination or substitution methods to resolve all the equations.

Step 7 – Check your final answers to see if they make sense with the information given in the problem.

For example, if the word problem involves a discount, the final price should be less or if a product was taxed then the final answer has to cost more.

TYPES OF WORD PROBLEMS

Word problems can be classified into 12 types. Below are examples of each type with a complete solution. Some types of word problems can be solved quickly using multiple choice strategies and some cannot. Always look for ways to estimate the answer and then eliminate choices.

1. Distance or speed

Two boats travel down a river towards the same destination, starting at the same time. One boat is traveling at 52 km/hr, and the other boat at 43 km/hr. How far apart will they be after 40 minutes?

    a. 46.67 km
    b. 19.23 km
    c. 6.04 km
    d. 14.39 km

Solution: C

After 40 minutes, the first boat will have traveled = 52 km/hr x 40 minutes/60 minutes = 34.7 km
After 40 minutes, the second boat will have traveled = 43 km/hr x 40/60 minutes = 28.66 km
Difference between the two boats will be 34.7 km – 28.66 km = 6.04 km.

Multiple Choice Strategy

First estimate the answer. The first boat is traveling 9 km. faster than the second, for 40 minutes, which is 2/3 of an hour. 2/3 of 9 = 6, as a rough guess of the distance apart.

Choices A, B and D can be eliminated right away.

2. Ratio

The instructions in a cookbook state that 700 grams of flour must be mixed in 100 ml of water, and 0.90 grams of salt added. A cook however has just 325 grams of flour. What is the quantity of water and salt that he should use?

    a. 0.41 grams and 46.4 ml
    b. 0.45 grams and 49.3 ml
    c. 0.39 grams and 39.8 ml
    d. 0.25 grams and 40.1 ml

Solution: A

The Cookbook states 700 grams of flour, but the cook only has 325. The first step is to determine the percentage of flour he has 325/700 x 100 = 46.4%
That means that 46.4% of all other items must also be used.
46.4% of 100 = 46.4 ml of water
46.4% of 0.90 = 0.41 grams of salt.

Multiple Choice Strategy

The recipe calls for 700 grams of flour but the cook only has 325, which is just less than half, the quantity of water and salt are going to be about half.

Choices C and D can be eliminated right away. Choice B is very close so be careful. Looking closely at choice B, it is exactly half, and since 325 is slightly less than half of 700, it can't be correct.
Choice A is correct.

3. Percent

An agent received $6,685 as his commission for selling a property. If his commission was 13% of the selling price, how much was the property?

    a. $68,825
    b. $121,850
    c. $49,025
    d. $51,423

Solution: D

Let's assume that the property price is x
That means from the information given, 13% of x = 6,685

Solve for x,
x = 6685 x 100/13 = $51,423

Multiple Choice Strategy

The commission, 13%, is just over 10%, which is easier to work with. Round up $6685 to $6700, and multiple by 10 for an approximate answer. 10 X 6700 = $67,000. You can do this in your head. Choice B is much too big and can be eliminated. Choice C is too small and can be eliminated. Choices A and D are left and good possibilities.

Do the calculations to make the final choice.

4. Sales & Profit

A store owner buys merchandise for $21,045. He transports them for $3,905 and pays his staff $1,450 to stock the merchandise on his shelves. If he does not incur further costs, how much does he need to sell the items to make $5,000 profit?

    a. $32,500
    b. $29,350
    c. $32,400
    d. $31,400

Solution: D

Total cost of the items is $21,045 + $3,905 + $1,450 = $26,400
Total cost is now $26,400 + $5000 profit = $31,400

Multiple Choice Strategy

Round off and add the numbers up in your head quickly. 21,000 + 4,000 + 1500 = 26500. Add in 5000 profit for a total of 31500.

Choice B is too small and can be eliminated. Choice C and Choice A are too large and can be eliminated.

5. Tax/Income

A woman earns $42,000 per month and pays 5% tax on her monthly income. If the Government increases her monthly taxes by $1,500, what is her income after tax?

   a. $38,400
   b. $36,050
   c. $40,500
   d. $39, 500

Solution: A

Initial tax on income was 5/100 x 42,000 = $2,100
$1,500 was added to the tax to give $2,100 + 1,500 = $3,600
Income after tax is $42,000 - $3,600 = $38,400

6. Simple Interest

Simple interest is one type of interest problems. There are always four variables of any simple interest equation. With simple interest, you would be given three of these variables and be asked to solve for one unknown variable. With more complex interest problems, you would have to solve for multiple variables.

The four variables of simple interest are:

P – Principal which refers to the original amount of money put in the account
I – Interest or the amount of money earned as interest
r – Rate or interest rate. This MUST ALWAYS be in decimal format and not in percentage
t – Time or the amount of time the money is kept in the account to earn interest

The formula for simple interest is I = P x r x t

Example 1

A customer deposits $1,000 in a savings account with a bank that offers 2% interest. How much interest will be earned after 4 years?

For this problem, there are 3 variables as expected.

P = $1,000
t = 4 years
r = 2%
I = ?

Before we can begin solving for I using the simple interest formula, we need to first convert the rate from percentage to decimal.

2% = 2/100 = 0.02
Now we can use the formula: I = P x r x t

I = 1,000 x 0.02 x 4 = 80
This means that the $1,000 would have earned an interest of $80 after 4 years. The total in the account after 4 years will thus be principal + interest earned, or 1,000 + 80 = $1,080

Example 2

Sandra deposits $1400 in a savings account with a bank at 5% interest. How long will she have to leave the money in the bank to earn $420 as interest to buy a second-hand car?

In this example, the given information is:
I = $420
P = $1,400

r - 5%
t - ?
As usual, first we convert the rate from percentage to decimal
5% = 5/100 = 0.05

Next, we plug in the variables we know into the simple interest formula - I = P x r x t

420 = 1,400 x 0.05 x t
420 = 70 x t
420 = 70t
t = 420/70
t = 6

Sandra will have to leave her $1,400 in the bank for 6 years to earn her an interest of $420 at a rate of 5%.

Other important simple interest formula to remember

To use this formula below, do not convert r (rate) to decimal.

P = 100 x interest/ r x t
r = 100 x interest/p x t
t = 100 x interest/ p x r

7. Averaging

The average weight of 10 books is 54 grams. 2 more books were added and the average weight became 55.4. If one of the 2 new books added weighed 62.8 g, what is the weight of the other?

    a. 44.7 g
    b. 67.4 g
    c. 62 g
    d. 52 g

Solution: C

Total weight of 10 books with average 54 grams will be = 10 × 54 = 540 g
Total weight of 12 books with average 55.4 will be = 55.4 × 12

= 664.8 g
So total weight of the remaining 2 will be= 664.8 − 540 = 124.8 g
If one weighs 62.8, the weight of the other will be= 124.8 g − 62.8 g = 62 g

Multiple Choice Strategy

Averaging problems can be estimated by looking at which direction the average goes. If additional items are added and the average goes up, the new items much be greater than the average. If the average goes down after new items are added, the new items must be less than the average.

Here, the average is 54 grams and 2 books are added which increases the average to 55.4, so the new books must weight more than 54 grams.

Choices A and D can be eliminated right away.

8. Probability

A bag contains 15 marbles of various colors. If 3 marbles are white, 5 are red and the rest are black, what is the probability of randomly picking out a black marble from the bag?

    a. 7/15
    b. 3/15
    c. 1/5
    d. 4/15

Solution: A

Total marbles = 15
Number of black marbles = 15 − (3 + 5) = 7
Probability of picking out a black marble = 7/15

9. Geometry

The length of a rectangle is 5 in. more than its width. The perimeter of the rectangle is 26 in. What is the width and length of the rectangle?

    a. width = 6 inches, Length = 9 inches
    b. width = 4 inches, Length = 9 inches
    c. width =4 inches, Length = 5 inches
    d. width = 6 inches, Length = 11 inches

Solution: B

Formula for perimeter of a rectangle is 2(L + W)
p=26, so 2(L+W) = p
The length is 5 inches more than the width, so
2(w+5) + 2w = 26
2w + 10 + 2w = 26
2w + 2w = 26 - 10
4w = 16

W = 16/4 = 4 inches

L is 5 inches more than w, so L = 5 + 4 = 9 inches.

10. Totals and fractions

A basket contains 125 oranges, mangos and apples. If 3/5 of the fruits in the basket are mangos and only 2/5 of the mangos are ripe, how many ripe mangos are there in the basket?

    a. 30
    b. 68
    c. 55
    d. 47

Solution: A
Number of mangos in the basket is 3/5 x 125 = 75
Number of ripe mangos = 2/5 x 75 = 30

LOGIC

THIS SECTION CONTAINS A SELF-ASSESSMENT AND LOGIC TUTORIALS. The Tutorials are designed to familiarize general principles and the self-assessment contains general questions similar to the number operations questions likely to be on the PSEE exam, but are not intended to be identical to the exam questions and are for skill practice only. The tutorials are not designed to be a complete logic course, and it is assumed that students have some familiarity with logic. If you do not understand parts of the tutorial, or find the tutorial difficult, it is recommended that you seek out additional instruction.

Logic Self-Assessment

Below is a number operations self-assessment. The purpose of the self-assessment is:

- Identify your strengths and weaknesses.
- Develop your personalized study plan (above)
- Get accustomed to the PSEE format
- Extra practice – the self-assessments are almost a full 3rd practice test!

The questions below are not the same as you will find on the PSEE - that would be too easy! And nobody knows what the questions will be and they change all the time. Below are general logic questions that cover the same areas as the PSEE. So, while the format and exact wording of the questions may differ slightly, and change from year to year, if you can answer the questions below, you will have no problem with the logic section of the PSEE.

The self-assessment is designed to give you a baseline score in the different areas covered. Here is a brief outline of how your score on the self-assessment relates to your understanding of the material.

75% - 100%	Excellent – you have mastered the content
50 – 75%	Good. You have a working knowledge. Even though you can just pass this section, you may want to review the tutorials and do some extra practice to see if you can improve your mark.
25% - 50%	Below Average. You do not understand the content. Review the tutorials, and retake this quiz again in a few days, before proceeding to the rest of the practice test questions.
Less than 25%	Poor. You have a very limited understanding. Please review the Tutorials, and retake this quiz again in a few days, before proceeding to the rest of the practice test questions.

Self-Assessment Answer Sheet

	A	B	C	D
1	○	○	○	○
2	○	○	○	○
3	○	○	○	○
4	○	○	○	○
5	○	○	○	○
6	○	○	○	○
7	○	○	○	○
8	○	○	○	○
9	○	○	○	○
10	○	○	○	○

1. The Silver fish can swim faster than the black fish. The gold fish can swim faster than the black fish. The gold fish can swim faster than the silver fish.

If the first 2 statements are true, then the third statement is:

    a. True
    b. False
    c. Uncertain

2. All rabbits have fur. Some rabbits are pets. Some pets have fur. If the first 2 statements are true, then the third statement is:

    a. True
    b. False
    c. Uncertain

3. Deciduous trees drop their leaves in the fall. Conifers keep their leaves all year round. Conifers are deciduous. If the first 2 statements are true, then the third statement is:

    a. True
    b. False
    c. Uncertain

4. No homework is fun. Reading is homework. Reading is not fun. If the first 2 statements are true, then the third statement is:

    a. True
    b. False
    c. Uncertain

5. All informative things are useful things. Some websites are not useful things. Some websites are not informative. If the first 2 statements are true, then the third statement is:

   a. True
   b. False
   c. Uncertain

ANALYTICAL REASONING

6. For this question, use your knowledge of the real relations between the existing nouns to determine the best response.

A CRUX resembles LILO but is closer to the Sun
A TIGO resembles Jupiter but is farther from the Sun
A LILO resembles Earth but is closer to the Sun

Which of the following is correct?

   a. LILO is farther from the Sun than Jupiter
   b. CRUX is closer to the Sun than Jupiter
   c. Jupiter is closer to the Sun than LILO
   d. LILO is farther from the Sun than TIGO

7. For this question, use your knowledge of the real relations between the existing nouns to determine the best response.

A CUXA is stronger than iron
A BUXA is weaker than wood
A SAMSA is weaker than BUXA

Which of the following is correct?

    a. CUXA is not the strongest
    b. BUXA is weaker than iron
    c. SAMSA is not the weakest
    d. None of the above

8. For this question, use your knowledge of the real relations between the existing nouns to determine the best response.

A DJANGO resembles a watermelon but is heavier
A VANGO resembles an apple but is lighter
A TANGO resembles a DJANGO but is heavier

Which of the following is correct?

    a. DJANGO weighs less than an apple
    b. VANGO weighs as much as TANGO
    c. TANGO is the heaviest
    d. None of the above

9. For this question, use your knowledge of the real relations between the existing nouns to determine the best response.

KAKA is thicker than milk
SUKA is of same thickness as water
BUKA is thinner than water

Which of the following is correct?

    a. SUKA is the thinnest
    b. BUKA is thicker than milk
    c. milk is thicker than SUKA
    d. KAKA is not the thickest

10. For this question, use your knowledge of the real relations between the existing nouns to determine the best response.

NONO is longer than meter
BONO is smaller than micron
SONO is longer than BONO

Which of the following is correct?

  a. BONO is the smallest
  b. NONO is the longest
  c. SONO is the longest
  d. SONO is smaller than nano

Answer Key

1. Uncertain
We don't have enough information here to make a decision. Perhaps the gold fish can swim faster than the black fish AND the silver fish – we don't know.

2. True
This argument is a little sloppy, because the 2nd statement and the conclusion both use 'some.' However, it is a valid argument.

3. False
This is a clearly false argument.

4. True
This is a very strong argument. If the first two statement are true, then the third statement or conclusion must be true.

5. True
This is a strong argument since the first statement uses 'all,' and the second statement uses 'some.' And the conclusion uses 'some.'

6. B
Based on the relations outlined in the first & third statements, we know that a CRUX is closer to the Sun than a LILO, which is closer than Earth. We also know that Earth is closer than Jupiter from the knowledge we have of these existing nouns, and, from the second statement, we know that Jupiter is closer than a TIGO. From closest to farthest, the order of the words is: CRUX, LILO, Earth, Jupiter, TIGO. Therefore, choice B is the correct answer.

[CRUX<LILO<Earth<Jupiter<TIGO in terms of distance from the Sun]

7. B
Based on real relations, iron is stronger than wood. From the first statement, we know CUXA is stronger than iron which is stronger than wood. From second statement, we know that BUXA is weaker than wood, and therefore weaker than iron and CUXA. From third statement, we know that SAMSA is

weaker than BUXA and therefore weaker than other three as well. From weakest to strongest, the order of the words is: SAMSA, BUXA, wood, iron, CUXA. Therefore, choice B is correct.

[SAMSA<BUXA<wood<iron<CUXA in STRENGTH]

8. C
A watermelon is heavier than an apple based on real relations. From first statement, we see that DJANGO is heavier than watermelon which is heavier than an apple. From third statement, we know that TANGO is heavier than Django (and therefore heaviest) while, from second statement, we know that VANGO is lighter than apple (and therefore lightest). From lightest to heaviest, the order of the words is VANGO, apple, watermelon, DJANGO, TANGO. Therefore choice C is correct.

[TANGO>DJANGO>watermelon>apple>VANGO in weight]

9. C
Based on real relations, milk is thicker than water. From first and second statements, KAKA is thicker than milk, which is thicker than water, which is of same thickness as SUKA. From third statement, BUKA is thinner than water and therefore the lightest. From heaviest to thinnest, the order of the words is KAKA, milk, water & SUKA, BUKA. Therefore choice C is correct.

[KAKA>milk>water=SUKA>BUKA]

10. A
Based on real relations, meter is longer than a micron (1 meter = million microns). From first statement, NONO is longer than meter ,which is longer than micron. From second statement, micron is longer than BONO. From third statement, SONO is longer than BONO, making BONO the smallest. Relationship between SONO and NONO is unclear.

Therefore choice A is correct. All other choices are inconclusive.

Logic - A Quick Tutorial

Understanding syllogism can be tricky which is why it's important to understand the strategies involved in solving the problems. Here are some tips to guide you when reviewing for syllogism exam questions:

Logical syllogisms have three key components: the major premise, minor premise, and the conclusion. Practicing logic questions helps you identify these quickly and easily.

There are two terms used in each part, which can be understood through the form ""Some/all A is/are [not] B." Each premise has a common term with the conclusion as seen in the example below:
Premise: All birds are animals
Premise: All parrots are birds
Conclusion: All parrots are animals

In this example, "animal" is the major term and predicate of the conclusion, "parrot" is the minor term and subject of the conclusion, and "bird" is the middle term.

Clearly, this argument is rock-solid. If ALL birds are animals, AND all parrots are birds, then the conclusion must be true – All parrots must be animals.

To check on this, let's try a variation:

Some birds are animals.
All parrots are birds
All parrots are animals.

Clearly, this is not true. If only 'some' birds are animals, then there are some birds which are NOT animals, and we don't have any information about if the 'some' birds which are not animals. Perhaps the 'some birds that are not animals' are parrots, and perhaps not.

Here is another example:

This store only sells used textbooks.

My textbook is used.
My textbook came from that store.

This is clearly a not true. We do not know if the store is the only store in the world that sells textbooks, so clearly the textbook in question could have come from that store or any other store.

STRUCTURE

There are four possible variations to each "Some/all/no A is/are [not] B," structure.

All birds are animals.
All parrots are birds.
All parrots are animals.

Clearly a very solid argument – IF all birds are animals AND all parrots are birds, then the conclusion, all parrots are animals MUST be true.

Here is a variation that is NOT true:

Some birds are animals.
All parrots are birds.
All parrots are animals.

Here we don't know if the 'some' birds that are NOT animals includes parrots or not. They may be but we don't know.

Here is the negative example:

No birds are foxes.
All parrots are birds.
No parrots are foxes.

A very good argument where the conclusion, No parrots are foxes MUST be true if the premises are true.

Notice what happens if we substitute 'some' into the

argument.

Some birds are foxes.
All parrots are birds.
No parrots are foxes.

No birds are foxes.
Some parrots are birds.
No parrots are foxes.

Both of these are clearly false. The argument relies on the fact the absolute statements ALL and NONE.

Using some can give a very solid argument though. Consider these:
All dogs are animals.
Some mammals are dogs.
Some mammals are animals.

No dogs are birds.
Some mammals are dogs.
Some mammals are not birds.

No restaurant food is healthy.
Some recipes are healthy.
Some recipes are not restaurant foods.

All liars are evildoers.
Some doctors are not evildoers.
Some doctors are not liars.

All these are very good arguments where the conclusion MUST be true if the premises are true.

Below is a comprehensive list of all valid logic argument forms. Study these forms and make sure that you are familiar with them and understand why the conclusion must be true.

The Real World

Generally, exam questions are not exactly like the forms we have been discussing so far, but are similar. Understanding the correct forms is still very important and necessary to understanding the underlying structure.
Here are some example logic questions:

1.
Practice makes perfect.
I am perfect.
I practiced a lot.

If the first 2 statements are true, then the third statement is:

True   False   Uncertain

The correct answer is - Uncertain. There are all sorts of reasons you could be perfect without practicing. For example, you could be perfect looking, or your hair could be perfect, or you could be perfect by a coincidence.

2.
People who smoke cigarettes have a 75% chance of getting cancer.

I have cancer.
I smoked a lot.

If the first 2 statements are true, then the third statement is:

True   False   Uncertain

The correct answer is - Uncertain. There are many reasons you could have cancer. In addition, you may be among the 25% of people who smoke and do NOT get cancer.

3.
Most car accidents happen in the morning.
I don't drive in the morning.
I am unlikely to have an accident.
If the first 2 statements are true, then the third statement is:

True   False   Uncertain
The correct answer is - Uncertain.

4.
Halibut are a large fish.
I caught a small fish.
I did not catch a halibut.
If the first 2 statements are true, then the third statement is:

True   False   Uncertain

The correct answer is – False. You could have caught a baby halibut. In order for this to be true, you would have to say,

All halibut are large fish.
I caught a small fish.
I did not catch a halibut.
Here, the first premise is ALL halibut are large, which would include baby halibut, so if the first two premises are true, the third statement MUST be true also.

A Different Style

Here is a different style of question.

1.
Angel gets the highest grades in all the subjects in school. She is also the president of the Student Council. Every year she gets the highest award given by the school.

   a. Angel is a slow learner.

   b. Everybody admires Angel.

   c. Other children are envious of Angel.

   d. Angel is at the top of her class.

Let's look at the choices. Choice A is clearly false. Choice B, may be true but it also may not be true – no information is given. It is likely that everyone admires her, but we don't know that for sure. The same with choice C. Probably other students are envious of her, but we don't know that for sure

and no information is given. She could, for example, have rigged the election for Student Council and cheated on all her exams and everyone hates her!
Choice D is correct – This we do now for sure.

2.
Students enjoy playing football after school. Sometimes, they play basketball with other kids. On weekends, they play baseball, badminton, or tennis.

    a. Students prefer playing indoors.

    b. Students enjoy different kinds of sports.

    c. Students hate playing.

    d. Playing is a form of exercise.

The correct answer is B. The only certain thing is children enjoy different kinds of sports. For choice A, no information is given if they are playing indoors or outdoors. Choice C is probably false, but we don't know. Choice D is true, but not related to the information given. Choice D is designed to confuse.

LIST OF ALL VALID LOGIC ARGUMENT FORMS

All men are fallible.
All men are animals.
Some animals are fallible.

Some books are precious.
All books are perishable.
Some perishable things are precious.

All books are imperfect.
Some books are informative.
Some informative things are imperfect.

No snakes are good to eat.
All snakes are animals.
Some animals are not good to eat.

Some websites are not helpful.
All websites are internet resources.

Some internet resources are not helpful.
No lepers are allowed to enter the church.
All lepers are human.
Some humans are not allowed to enter the church.

All pigs are unclean.
All unclean things are best avoided.
Some things that are best avoided are pigs.

All trees are plants.
No plants are birds.
No birds are trees.

Some evil doers are lawyers.
All lawyers are human.
Some humans are evil doers.

No meals are free.
All free things are desirable.
Some desirable things are not meals.

No dogs are birds.
Some birds are pets.
Some pets are not dogs.

Situational Judgement

This section contains Situational Judgement practice questions. So, while the self-assessment contains general questions similar to the situational judgement questions likely to be on the PSEE, but are not intended to be identical to the exam questions.

Situational judgement questions test your judgement, not what you memorize. The best way to study for this type of question is to practice, using your best judgement.

The questions below are not the same as you will find on the PSEE - that would be too easy! And nobody knows what the questions will be and they change all the time. Mostly the changes consist of substituting new questions for old, but the changes can be new question formats or styles, changes to the number of questions in each section, changes to the time limits for each section and combining sections. So, while the format and exact wording of the questions may differ slightly, and change from year to year, if you can answer the questions below, you will have no problem with the situational judgement section of the PSEE.

Situational Judgement Self-Assessment

Situational Judgement Tests generally cover the following areas in the given scenarios:

- Communication
- Being a Team Player
- Building Relationships
- Organization and Planning

- Focus on the Customer

- Analytical and Creative Thinking

Once complete, use the table below to assess your understanding of the content, and prepare your study schedule described in chapter 1.

80% - 100%	Excellent – you have mastered the content!
60 – 79%	Good. You have a working knowledge. Even though you can just pass this section, you may want to review the Tutorials and do some extra practice to see if you can improve your mark.
40% - 59%	Below Average. You do not understand Situational judgement problems. Review the tutorials, and retake this quiz again in a few days, before proceeding to the rest of the study guide.
Less than 40%	Poor. You have a very limited understanding of Situational judgement problems. Please review the Tutorials, and retake this quiz again in a few days, before proceeding to the rest of the study guide.

Answer Sheet

	A	B	C	D
1	○	○	○	○
2	○	○	○	○
3	○	○	○	○
4	○	○	○	○
5	○	○	○	○
6	○	○	○	○
7	○	○	○	○
8	○	○	○	○
9	○	○	○	○
10	○	○	○	○
11	○	○	○	○
12	○	○	○	○
13	○	○	○	○
14	○	○	○	○
15	○	○	○	○
16	○	○	○	○
17	○	○	○	○
18	○	○	○	○
19	○	○	○	○
20	○	○	○	○

Scenario 1

You have assigned your team some work with a tight deadline which, unless met, means that the company is going to incur huge losses. You assign Jackie is to lead the team delivering the assignment. Two days before the deadline, Jackie shows up in your office and explains to you that it will not be possible to deliver the project on time because one of the team members failed to play his part.

How are you going to handle the situation?

    a. Quarrel with Jackie and blame the delay on her entirely as a team leader.

    b. Brainstorm with her on what may be done

    c. Ensure that both Jackie and the employee get a salary cut

    d. Call a meeting and shame the entire team for failing.

Scenario 2

A customer calls in with a list of complaints about your company. The sales representative directs the client to your office. The customer is angry and dissatisfied with their purchases.

How do you communicate to the dissatisfied customer?

    a. Explain to the customer why they are wrong and how right your argument is

    b. Listen carefully to the complaint without interrupting, show empathy and understanding and offer the best assistance you can.

    c. Blame the customer for not reading the terms and conditions of purchase

    d. Deny a refund and refer the customer to another company.

Scenario 3

A lot of shipments have been directed to your department which is currently short-staffed. The supervisor asks all employees to take turns working overtime to handle the situation. You feel worn-out having worked late more than once during the week. You and your friends have plans to go out on Friday evening but your supervisor asks you to cover for a sick colleague.

How should you respond?

    a. Explain to the supervisor that those plans are hard to change because you waited two summers to re-unite with your college friends.

    b. Accept the work and turn your friends down.

    c. Ignore the order and go out anyway.

    d. Communicate with your team members and supervisor and weigh the issues at hand and act accordingly.

Scenario 4

You have been working with a company for more than three years. During this period, you have familiarized yourself with all polices governing the company's operations. On this particular day, your immediate supervisor asks you to undertake a task which definitely goes against company policies.

What should you do?

    a. Do as the supervisor asks and disregard the company policies

    b. Decline to do what the supervisor asks of you.

    c. Explain to the supervisor that the action goes against the policies

    d. Ask the supervisor whether he knows the policies of the company

Scenario 5

You are working on a task that calls for skills that you don't have. You need help from your work mates who have the required skills.

How would you go about seeking collaboration?

> a. Make a thorough analysis of all the parameters at play and act decisively.
>
> b. Ask for collaboration from other team members.
>
> c. Act immediately without thinking.
>
> d. Fail to take any action.

Scenario 6

One project assigned to you involves a client, Jane. She keeps calling you to make changes to the original plan. It is your feeling that she is changing most of the projects specifics which could directly impact the budget.

How should you deal with this situation?

> a. Propose that she makes all changes in an official manner, through letters and email.
>
> b. Take her orders and do as she pleases to ensure customer satisfaction.
>
> c. Refuse to do what she asks outside of the initial contract/agreement/project.
>
> d. Discuss this matter with your superiors and find a way forward.

Scenario 7

A client is very much opposed to your point of view while trying to explain something to him. It is important that they are convinced about the idea you are putting across.

How would you go about making the client see things from your perspective?

    a. Begin with understanding and seeing things in your client's perspective.

    b. Begin with explaining your point of view to the client in clear and simple terms.

    c. Decode what your client could be thinking about

    d. Sit the client down and prove to him why he is wrong

Scenario 8

Conflict in the workplace is common in most organizations. Your co-worker falsely accuses you and you feel resentment towards him. The two of you get into an extended conflict and antagonistic relationship, which could see production affected.

How should you handle this situation?

    a. Apologize to your coworker.

    b. Have a supervisor involved in resolving the conflict.

    c. Act normal and pretend that nothing wrong will happen.

    d. Ask for an apology from your friend.

Scenario 9

You are on shift and performing your normal duties, when something very urgent comes up. The issue is extremely demanding and none of your colleagues have handled this type of situation before.

How should you handle this situation?

a. Make a thorough analysis of all the parameters at play and act decisively.

b. Ask for collaboration from other team members on the appropriate course of action.

c. Act immediately without thinking

d. Fail to take any action

Scenario 10

It's a bright Monday morning and you show up to work as usual. Before you get to the main door, you over-hear your team members shouting and yelling at each other. It seems like a really big fight is going on. It's obvious that your co-workers disagree on some very basic principles.

How should you go about bringing cohesion to your team?

a. Refer this matter to your supervisor

b. Ask what could be wrong and offer advice

c. Talk to each of the employees separately

d. Discuss this with the entire team and ask for solutions

Scenario 11

As a department head, you propose new procedure and you are sure it will improve the work process. Some of the employee in the department oppose it. One of your subordinates criticizes the procedure to your direct boss.

What action would you take?

a. You choose not to respond to prevent the situation to escalating into a conflict.

b. You punish that person for skipping protocol and going to your boss and work to promote the idea more enthusiastically.

c. You invite the employee for a discussion and explain to him that bypassing your authority cannot be tolerated.

d. You decide to keep your employees satisfied by implementing the idea in part to maintain the employees trust in you as their manager.

Scenario 12

At a strategy meeting with your direct supervisor and the marketing manager, your find yourself in the middle of a conflict between them. You understand that the two are always in constant conflict and do not get along professionally. They are asking you to pick a side about the strategies for a new campaign.

What should you do?

a. You go with the marketing managers idea since she is senior it would be safer and politically wiser to support her as she has more influence on the future of your career.

b. You accept your supervisor's idea since he is directly above you and directly influences your daily routine which makes it politically correct to side with him.

c. You measure the advantages and disadvantages of both sides and make a decision without getting involved in their personal conflict.

d. You believe that choosing a side will negatively impact your career since both sides are superior to you. You refuse to pick a side and say both strategies are equally successful.

Scenario 13

After serving for two years as the sales manager, a new deputy manager is appointed by the director. You however find her disloyal and arrogant in many ways. You discover the director is considering an opportunity for her in a different position after this. The downside, is this would speed up her promotion.

What should you do?

a. Since she will eventually relocate, you encourage and approve her participation in the course.

b. You contact your director and recommend she be relocated to another position best suited to her capabilities.

c. You approve her participation and take time to discuss it with her. You honestly express your concerns and work out your differences and update your director.

d. You blindly approve her participation since it was offered by the director. You voice your concerns to the director separately.

Scenario 14

For the past year you have worked as a salesperson and have consistently hit sales targets. Recently, for personal reasons you haven't been focused and haven't been making sales targets. Changes in the market are also a factor, decreasing your sales by a significant margin. Your director does not seem to understand the changes in the market and is blaming you for the reduction in sales figures.

What should you do?

a. Talk to your director about your personal situation and apologize for the decline in the team's performance. Request for a few days off to put your house in order.

b. You decide to put your personal issues aside and consult other sales directors on how they deal with the changes in the market place. You fully dedicate yourself to your work.

c. You update your director on the market changes. You explain to him that changing or improving sales with the current conditions is beyond your ability.

d. You decide to put pressure on your team scolding them for the poor performance. You go ahead and set new targets with the market changes in mind.

Scenario 15

You have been working in the same company for 3 years and have successfully risen through the ranks. You now have the feeling that you have reached your potential in the company and start pursuing options to advance your career in other organizations. You are currently negotiating a new contract and rumors that you are switching jobs are spreading fast in your company.

What should you do?

> a. You decide that since the rumor is already out, you update everyone of your ongoing negotiations in the new company. You do this as it may even push your current directors to give you a promotion in the current company.
>
> b. Since nothing has been decided yet and it is still a rumor you maintain your silence on the issue until you give notice.
>
> c. Since you will probably leave and the rumor is already out, you invest less and less in your current position and invest more time in getting the new position.
>
> d. Since the rumor is out, you address your manager's doubts by updating him of your intentions of leaving and keep working normally since you are still an employee.

Scenario 16

The company you work for is having financial problems. You have come up with an innovative way to get more clients. The downside is the company will have to give up a loyal but less profitable client due to a conflict of interest. A few people on the marketing team agree with you, but your manager has a different opinion as he thinks the move is too risky.

What should you do?

a. You withdraw your proposition as you trust your managers judgement and believe there is no reason to go against his judgement.

b. You present a document that details the benefits your proposition will bring to the organization, but support his decision if he insists on it.

c. You implement the idea despite your managers resistance as you have a lot of faith in the proposition. You trust your gut and implement the idea behind your manager's back for the companies benefit.

d. You confront your manager and insist the idea is the best way out. You believe you are right you take the support of the marketing team and push your manager until he is convinced you are right.

Scenario 17

You are being undermined by a co-worker that has a junior position to you and has not been working there as long as you. He is, however, considered a fast learner and is more educated than you. You get information from someone that the co-worker is interested in taking over your some of your roles.

What should you do?

a. Wait to see how it turns out as all this is hearsay and you consider it rumors.

b. You call the co-worker and talk to them, letting them know that cooperation is essential in any organization and you have something to learn form each other. You say that you will take more serious action if he refuses to understand.

c. You treat the matter with seriousness taking no chances. Your report your co-worker to your supervisor and advise him to replace the co-worker.

d. Since you don't want to turn the matter into a big issue, you seek the help of a third party in telling your co-worker that their behavior cannot be tolerated.

Scenario 18

You are the manager of a department where two members are long overdue to participate in a professional training course. The training manager lets you know that she has opted for individuals from a different department for the training. You do not have a good relationship with the training department.

a. You reject the training manager's decision with a furious email demanding she re-opens the training as your employee's performance will be affected by their lack of training. You cc the email to the director.

b. You wait for the next training since your relationship with the training manager is already very poor.

c. You contact the manager of the other department and request a slot for one of your employees in the two slots he has been given.

d. You talk to the training manager to understand the reasons for her decision. You explain the importance of the training to your department and why it is necessary that your employee take it.

Scenario 19

One of your employees has shown significant decline in sales in the past month. Although this decline has been happening for a while, it has significantly increased in the past two weeks. In addition, the employee has been coming to work late and seems frustration in her work. Since she is a popular employee who has been working at the company for 2 years, her behavior is influencing the work atmosphere.

What should you do?

a. Explain to her that her behavior is not just affecting not only her performance, her but the entire office. You express your intentions to help her through whatever she's going through on condition she improves her attitude.

b. Since she is a popular employee you feel it necessary to replace her temporarily to prevent a decline in office performance. You assign her back office tasks and assure her she will have her role back if her performance improves.

c. You schedule a staff meeting to discus the negative attitude you in the office. You point out the problematic employee and talk about how she is affecting the office atmosphere hoping she will change.

d. You let it blow over. Since she has consistently proved to be a good employee you feel no need to reprimand her. Part of your job is to accommodate employees when they face challenging situations.

Scenario 20

You are assigned a joint project with a co-worker who has been working in the department longer than you have. He does not put in much effort as he lacks the motivation to develop professionally.

What should you do?

a. You accept the situation as it is and share the workload to the best of your ability. You leave the rest up to him.

b. You are concerned that poor quality work will effect your reputation and the company's reputation negatively and decide to put in extra hours to complete personally the project in the best way you can.

c. You contact your manger to report the situation as you cannot tolerate this attitude. You request the co-worker be replaced for the project.

d. You talk to the co-worker and negotiate that the work be distributed fairly between the two of you. You however consider the fact that you might have to put in extra effort to complete the project.

ANSWER KEY

1. B
What has happened in the past is hard to reverse and instead of wasting more time, a good leader would first, work towards meeting the requirements. In this given scenario, the possibility of incurring losses would be blamed on you. The most correct thing to do therefore is to brainstorm with Jackie and the rest of the team on what may be done by each member to meet the deadline.

Choices A, C and D will lead to resentment against the company and yourself and would be bad for moral. The object is to avoid loss and complete the project.

2. B
Effective communication is two-sided. Before you respond to the client's complaint, it is important to understand the complaint. Listen carefully and break down each important factor. Without proper listening, you are bound to misunderstand and irritate the client further. This way you end up losing clients. Be empathetic in your response and make yourself easy to understand.

Most people are naturally inclined to thinking that they are always correct in their thinking. This natural bias causes people to feel bad whenever they are proven wrong by someone. Choice A could seem appropriate, but it is detrimental for the future of the business. Most people blame everything on everyone but themselves. When you blame them, choice C, they are less likely to become loyal customers and your business loses in the long run. Choice D is obviously incorrect and can be eliminated right away.

3. D
Communication is very essential in any business undertaking. It is important to tell your side of the story as well as listen to deliberations by the team members. Consultations lead to better decision making.

Choice A seems appropriate; however, it fails to account for the supervisor's point of view or argument. However valid your argument might be, it is not sufficient to solve the issue. Going to work unwillingly (choice B) on the other hand is bad for you and for the company as well. You won't be able to concentrate and your productivity will be affected. Finding common ground or some type of accommodation is the best thing to do.

4. C
It is possible the supervisor is unaware of a policy. It therefore becomes important to speak with them politely.

Rarely are supervisors wrong. However sometimes unexpected things happen, but that does not allow you to do something you know violates company policy (Choice A). Declining to do the task (Choice B) without explanation is not likely to be taken well by your superior. Generally supervisors know the policies better than you although it is possible (Choice D). Choice C is the better choice.

5. B
Two heads are better than one. By allowing others to have an input in the final decision, you not only reduce unnecessary resistance but also increase employee commitment. To be effective, a leader should ensure team members are part of the decision-making process. Being involved gives them a sense of importance and belonging.

It is possible to make a thorough analysis of the factors involved in this and assume that one is able to make a decision that will be accepted by all (Choice A) however getting buy-in from everyone is a better strategy. Choices C and D are Obviously wrong choices and can be eliminated right away.

6. D
Some things are beyond your capacity as an employee, and above your pay-grade. Whether it comes from the client or from other colleagues some issues need to be forwarded to your superiors. By directing Jane to your superiors you will have drawn a line in the chain of command. You will have presented the company with appropriate information for them to make an informed decision.

You cannot accept or refuse to meet the new demands from

the client as you don't have the authority (choices B and C). Communicating in an official way is important for documentation purposes. By asking the client to write letters and email, (choice A) evidence for financial accounting is availed. However, it should not stop there.

7. A
Unless you first understand the viewpoint of your client, it will be very difficult to show them otherwise. By showing the client that you understand his problem, he is much likely to agree with you at some point.

It's not possible to read the mind of the other person, at least in practice. Unless you listen to the client, decoding his thoughts will be a great challenge to you (choice C). Choice B suggests a noble solution to the problem but fails to address the fundamental aspect of listening. Choice D is not an effective strategy - nobody like to be told they are wrong.

8. B
Involving a neutral person (the supervisor) in conflict resolution leads to better understanding amongst the discontented parties. By involving a third party, you can diffuse the situation quickly and amicably. The leader offers proper guidance and issues directions to safeguard the interests of the organization.

It is not a sure thing that issuing an apology would bring to an end of the conflict (choice A) – more than that is required. Similarly choice C, is not a solution, as it may be taken as an accusation.

9. B
The phrase, two heads are better than one is a full of psychological truth. Asking for collaboration from others gives you a better chance to analyze the situation and decide wisely. It also makes them feel valued which raises their commitment levels.

This is a good choice but choice B, asking for collaboration is better. Choices C and D, taking action without information, is dangerous to the business. It is similar to driving a car blindfolded. It is hard to make the right call when faced with a new challenge. Making decisions under pressure is a challenge to most leaders. Chances of error are so high that consulting is not an choice But a necessity.

10. A
Work-related conflict should be resolved by higher authority. An independent supervisor can provide the appropriate direction.

Choice D, discussing as a team and asking for solutions could deteriorate with members taking sides. Involve only the right people while solving such specific problems. Choice C, talking to each separately, may resolve but you are taking a chance you will not be able to resolve. Bringing it to you superiors is the best choice (choice A). Choice B, offering unsolicited advice would not be appreciated or resolve the situation.

11. C
Going over your head is disrespectful of your authority. Even though the new idea will make their work easier, some employees are resistant to change. Inviting them for a discussion demonstrates that you are serious about the idea and that you are available for discussions in case of a problem.

Ignoring the mistake, choice A, to avoid conflict will send a signal that you fear conflict. Punishing the employee, choice B, will probably cause resentment.

12. C
As a professional, you need to rise above personal conflict, even if others are not. Giving a professional opinion and risk going into the bad books of one of your superiors demonstrates that you are ready to risk personal gratification for the team's success.

Refusing to pick a side, or picking a side based on politics, might be a safe option to choose to a short-cited individual. This will not serve the organizational and both the manager and supervisor will be able to read your weakness in decision making. It will be clear to them you cannot make a decision for the benefit of the company.

13. C
This scenario has shown us that the deputy director is not incompetent but is arrogant and disloyal. This course will only improve her academic qualification but will not address he arrogance and disloyalty. Talking to her will open up her

mind to her weaknesses and give her a chance to reflect on them and correct. Informing the director will enable him find a solution to her weaknesses and find a way of helping her without compromising the company goals.

Approving her application without talking to her, (choice A) will only shift the problem from your department to the department she will be transferred to. Talking to the director without trying to address the issue first,(choice D), will not help her as she might lose the opportunity.

14. B
One should not allow their personal life to affect their professional life. To effectively cope with a volatile market, consult more experienced salespeople.

15. D
It is the responsibility of the employee to inform their manager of their intention to leave. This will help the manager in planning for the future. It will also give the manager a chance to address issues that might have caused you to look elsewhere for employment. It is also important to continue working normally as you are still an employee of the company you work for.

16. B
You need to try to convince the manager by educating him on the benefits of the idea backed by evidence without arguing with him in the presence of his subordinates. You also have a duty and obligation to support whatever decision the manager makes even if you believe you have a better idea.

17. B
By choosing choice B you will show honesty and genuine interest in the issue at hand. This serves the purpose of educating your co-worker on the benefits of cooperation. It is fair to take more action if the co-worker chooses to ignore your advice.

18. D
Choice D is the most effective. This might even give you a chance to sort out your strained relationship.

19. A

By selecting choice A as a manager, you have decided to solve the problem in a proactive way. Addressing the problem by talking to the employee will assure her that you care. As an employee that has consistently performed well talking to her will enable the manager get a better understanding of the problem she is facing and better help her.

Calling a staff meeting to address a personal problem, choice C, is a waste of time and a counter productive move. Publicly reprimanding a popular employee will only worsen the situation as she might feel offended. The employee might turn resentful and the hope that the behavior will improve might never come.

20. D

A joint project requires teamwork and team work requires communication and constant negotiation on what should be done and how it should be done. Negotiating and distributing the work fairly between the two of you will ensure he steps up and takes responsibility for his part of the project. However, because of the situation and poor performance will reflect badly on you as well, be prepared to put in some extra.

SEQUENCES

THIS SECTION CONTAINS A SELF-ASSESSMENT AND SEQUENCES TUTORIAL. The tutorial is designed to familiarize with general principles. So, while the self-assessment contains general questions similar to the sequences questions likely to be on the PSEE, but are not intended to be identical to the exam questions.

The questions below are not the same as you will find on the PSEE - that would be too easy! And nobody knows what the questions will be and they change all the time. Mostly the changes consist of substituting new questions for old, but the changes can be new question formats or styles, changes to the number of questions in each section, changes to the time limits for each section and combining sections. So, while the format and exact wording of the questions may differ slightly, and change from year to year, if you can answer the questions below, you will have no problem with the sequences section of the PSEE.

Once complete, use the table below to assess your understanding of the content, and prepare your study schedule described in chapter 1.

80% - 100%	Excellent – you have mastered the content!
60 – 79%	Good. You have a working knowledge. Even though you can just pass this section, you may want to review the Tutorials and do some extra practice to see if you can improve your mark.
40% - 59%	Below Average. You do not understand Sequences problems. Review the tutorials, and retake this quiz again in a few days, before proceeding to the rest of the study guide.
Less than 40%	Poor. You have a very limited understanding of Sequences problems. Please review the Tutorials, and retake this quiz again in a few days, before proceeding to the rest of the study guide.

Answer Sheet

	A	B	C	D
1	○	○	○	○
2	○	○	○	○
3	○	○	○	○
4	○	○	○	○
5	○	○	○	○
6	○	○	○	○
7	○	○	○	○
8	○	○	○	○
9	○	○	○	○
10	○	○	○	○
11	○	○	○	○
12	○	○	○	○
13	○	○	○	○
14	○	○	○	○
15	○	○	○	○
16	○	○	○	○
17	○	○	○	○
18	○	○	○	○
19	○	○	○	○
20	○	○	○	○

1. Consider the following sequence: 6, 12, 24, 48, ... What number should come next?

   a. 48
   b. 64
   c. 60
   d. 96

2. Consider the following sequence: 5, 6, 11, 17, ... What number should come next?

   a. 28
   b. 34
   c. 36
   d. 27

3. Consider the following sequence: 26, 21, ..., 11, 6. What is the missing number?

   a. 27
   b. 23
   c. 16
   d. 29

4. Consider the following sequence: L, O, R, ..., Y What is the missing letter?

   a. S
   b. U
   c. T
   d. M

5. Consider the following sequence: X, Z, B, D, ... What number should come next?

   a. E
   b. F
   c. G
   d. H

6. Consider the sequence in row A compared to row B. What is the missing number?

A	5	20	100	3	24
B	20	80	400	12	?

   a. 96
   b. 48
   c. 64
   d. 66

7. Consider the following sequence: L, N, P, R, ... What letter should come next?

   a. S
   b. T
   c. U
   d. V

8. Consider the following sequence: M, P, S, , Y. What is the missing letter?

   a. V
   b. T
   c. U
   d. X

9. Consider the following sequence:

   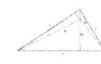   ???

a.    b. □   c. ☆

10. Consider the following sequence:

+ * + * | * + * + | * * + * | + + _ _

    a. + *
    b. * *
    c. + +
    d. * +

Answer Key

1. D
The numbers doubles each time.

2. A
Each number is the sum of the previous two numbers

3. C
The numbers decrease by 5 each time.

4. B
There are two letters missing between each one, so U is next.

5. B
Miss a letter each time and 'loop' back, so F is next.

6. A
The number in row B is 4 times the number in row A.

7. B
One letter is missing after each letter.

8. A
Two letters are missing after each letter.

9. B
The sequence shifts to the left each time, so the next figure will be the circle.

10. D
Each time the * and + alternate, either singly or doubles.

SEQUENCES TUTORIAL

Answering sequence questions is a skill of recognizing patterns, and the best way to improve is to familiarize yourself with the different types, and to practice. Here is a typical example:

Consider the following series: 26, 21, ..., 11, 6. What is the missing number?

   a. 27
   b. 23
   c. 16
   d. 29

Looking carefully at the sequence, we can see right away that each number is 5 less than the previous number, so the missing number is 16.

We can re-write this sequence in mathematical notation as, $a^1, a^2, a^3, ...$ an, where n is an integer and an is called its nth term. And we can write the sequence in the form of a formula, where an integer is substituted in the place of the variable in the formula and the terms are obtained.

For example, let us consider the sequence 5,10,15,20,...

- Here, $a^n = 5^n$. The formula $a^n = 5^n$.

- The nth term of a sequence can be found by plugging n into the formula for the sequence. So for example, if we wanted to find the 100th number in this sequence, we would substitute n=100 in the formula and get 500.

Types of Number Sequence Problems

1. Simple addition or subtraction – each number in the sequence is obtained by adding a number to the previous number.

For example, 2, 5, 8, 11, 14

Each number in the sequence is obtained by adding 3 to the previous number, which we could write as, $a^{n+1} = a^n + 3$.

2. Simple multiplication - each number in the sequence is obtained by multiplying the previous number by a whole number or fraction.

For example, 3, 6, 18, 54

Or,

20, 10, 5, 2.5

Each number in the first sequence is obtained by multiplying the previous number by 3, which we could write as, $a^{n+1} = a^n \times 3$.

In the second example, each number in the series is the previous number divided by 2, or multiplied by ½, or $a^{n+1} = a^n \times 1/2$.

3. Prime Numbers – each number in the sequence is a prime number.

For example,

23, ... , 31, 37

Answer: 29

4. Operations on the previous two numbers

For example,

8, 14, 22, 36, 58

Here the sequence is created by adding the previous 2 numbers.

5. Exponents

The number sequence is created by squaring or cubing each number.

For example,

3, 9, 81, 6561, where each number is squared.

6. Combining Sequences

2, 7, 13, 20, 28, 37

Here the sequence starts with 2, and each element is added to another sequence starting with 5. So, 2 + 5 = 7, 7 + 6 = 13, 13 + 7 = 20 and so on.

A variation is a sequence with a repeating element. For example,

1, 2, 3, 5, 7, 9, 12, 15

Here the sequence is, for each n, +1, +1, +1, +2, +2, +2, +3, +3,

7. Fractions

For example,

16/4, 4/2, 2/2, ½,

Fractions are often meant to confuse. If fractions don't have an obvious relationship, reduce them to lowest terms or to whole numbers. Reducing these to whole numbers, gives,

4, 2, 1, ½

Right away, we can see the numbers are half the previous number, so the next in the series is ¼.

In this example, the answer is a fraction; however, you may have to reduce fractions to see the relation, and then convert back to get the answer in the correct form.

Strategy for Answering Sequence Questions

Here is a quick method that will help you answer number series.

For example:

2, 5, 6, 7, 8,

Step 1 – glance at the series quickly and see if you can spot the pattern right away.

Step 2 – Start analyzing.

Take the different between the first 2 numbers and the different between the second 2 numbers.

2, (+3) 5, (+1) 6, (+1) 7, (+1)   8,

No clear pattern with a simple analysis. There is no addition, subtraction, multiplication, division, fractional or exponent relationship.

The relation must be a higher order or a second series.

Next look at the relation between the 1st number and the 2nd and the 1st and the 3rd.   We see that,

1st + 3 = 5, 1st + 4 = 6. That's it! The number 2 is added to the sequence, 3, 4, 5, 6, so the next number will be 2 + 7 = 9.

Practice Test Questions Set 1

The questions below are not the same as you will find on the PSEE - that would be too easy! And nobody knows what the questions will be and they change all the time. Below are general questions that cover the same subject areas as the PSEE. So, while the format and exact wording of the questions may differ slightly, and change from year to year, if you can answer the questions below, you will have no problem with the PSEE.

For the best results, take these practice test questions as if it were the real exam. Set aside time when you will not be disturbed, and a location that is quiet and free of distractions. Read the instructions carefully, read each question carefully, and answer to the best of your ability.

Use the bubble answer sheets provided. When you have completed the Practice Questions, check your answer against the Answer Key and read the explanation provided.

Do not attempt more than one set of practice test questions in one day. After completing the first practice test, wait two or three days before attempting the second set of questions.

Logic and Analytical Reasoning

	A	B	C	D	E		A	B	C	D	E
1	○	○	○	○	○	21	○	○	○	○	○
2	○	○	○	○	○	22	○	○	○	○	○
3	○	○	○	○	○	23	○	○	○	○	○
4	○	○	○	○	○	24	○	○	○	○	○
5	○	○	○	○	○	25	○	○	○	○	○
6	○	○	○	○	○	26	○	○	○	○	○
7	○	○	○	○	○	27	○	○	○	○	○
8	○	○	○	○	○	28	○	○	○	○	○
9	○	○	○	○	○	29	○	○	○	○	○
10	○	○	○	○	○	30	○	○	○	○	○
11	○	○	○	○	○						
12	○	○	○	○	○						
13	○	○	○	○	○						
14	○	○	○	○	○						
15	○	○	○	○	○						
16	○	○	○	○	○						
17	○	○	○	○	○						
18	○	○	○	○	○						
19	○	○	○	○	○						
20	○	○	○	○	○						

Situational Judgement

	A	B	C	D	E		A	B	C	D	E
1	○	○	○	○	○	21	○	○	○	○	○
2	○	○	○	○	○	22	○	○	○	○	○
3	○	○	○	○	○	23	○	○	○	○	○
4	○	○	○	○	○	24	○	○	○	○	○
5	○	○	○	○	○	25	○	○	○	○	○
6	○	○	○	○	○	26	○	○	○	○	○
7	○	○	○	○	○	27	○	○	○	○	○
8	○	○	○	○	○	28	○	○	○	○	○
9	○	○	○	○	○	29	○	○	○	○	○
10	○	○	○	○	○	30	○	○	○	○	○
11	○	○	○	○	○	31	○	○	○	○	○
12	○	○	○	○	○	32	○	○	○	○	○
13	○	○	○	○	○	33	○	○	○	○	○
14	○	○	○	○	○	34	○	○	○	○	○
15	○	○	○	○	○	35	○	○	○	○	○
16	○	○	○	○	○	36	○	○	○	○	○
17	○	○	○	○	○	37	○	○	○	○	○
18	○	○	○	○	○	38	○	○	○	○	○
19	○	○	○	○	○	39	○	○	○	○	○
20	○	○	○	○	○	40	○	○	○	○	○

SEQUENCES

	A	B	C	D
1	○	○	○	○
2	○	○	○	○
3	○	○	○	○
4	○	○	○	○
5	○	○	○	○
6	○	○	○	○
7	○	○	○	○
8	○	○	○	○
9	○	○	○	○
10	○	○	○	○
11	○	○	○	○
12	○	○	○	○
13	○	○	○	○
14	○	○	○	○
15	○	○	○	○
16	○	○	○	○
17	○	○	○	○
18	○	○	○	○
19	○	○	○	○
20	○	○	○	○

Problem Solving

	A	B	C	D
1	○	○	○	○
2	○	○	○	○
3	○	○	○	○
4	○	○	○	○
5	○	○	○	○
6	○	○	○	○
7	○	○	○	○
8	○	○	○	○
9	○	○	○	○
10	○	○	○	○
11	○	○	○	○
12	○	○	○	○
13	○	○	○	○
14	○	○	○	○
15	○	○	○	○

LOGIC

1. **Some cats have no tails. All cats are mammals. Some mammals have no tails.**

   If the first 2 statements are true, then the third statement is:

   a. True
   b. False
   c. Uncertain

2. **All students carry backpacks. My grandfather carries a backpack. Therefore, my grandfather is a student.**

   If the first 2 statements are true, then the third statement is:

   a. True
   b. False
   c. Uncertain

3. **All dogs are mammals. No cats are dogs. Therefore, no cats are mammals.**

   If the first 2 statements are true, then the third statement is:

   a. True
   b. False
   c. Uncertain

4. All cats are felines. All cats are mammals. All mammals are felines.

If the first 2 statements are true, then the third statement is:

   a. True
   b. False
   c. Uncertain

5. No mammals are fish. Some fish are not whales. Some whales are not mammals.

If the first 2 statements are true, then the third statement is:

   a. True
   b. False
   c. Uncertain

6. No fish are dogs, and no dogs can fly. All fish can fly.

If the first 2 statements are true, then the third statement is:

   a. True
   b. False
   c. Uncertain

7. All colonels are officers. All officers are soldiers. No colonels are soldiers.

If the first 2 statements are true, then the third statement is:

   a. True
   b. False
   c. Uncertain

8. Krizzia loves reading books. Nea enjoys playing with her dolls. Krizzia and Nea are cousins.

   a. Krizzia likes to play with Nea.

   b. Nea finds reading boring.

   c. Krizzia and Nea are blood related

   d. Nea and Krizzia are best friends.

9. The village is found in a coastal area. Many fishermen go out to sea everyday. They go home late in the afternoon.

   a. Fishing is the means of living of the villagers.

   b. Many fishermen hate fishing.

   c. Fishermen go out to sea especially in the evening.

   d. The village attracts tourists.

10. Ben and Ted are classmates. They would ride the school bus together. They also have lunch at the same table. They're even lab partners.

   a. Ben and Ted don't like each other.

   b. Ben prefers being with other children.

   c. Ben and Ted are inseparable.

   d. Ted is always alone.

11. Karen takes care of her garden everyday. She grows fruits and vegetables. She always waters them. She also pulls out the weeds and put fertilizer on her plants.

   a. Karen hates taking care of her plants.

   b. Karen is fond of gardening.

   c. Karen plants flowers in her garden.

   d. Karen and her mother work on the garden together.

12. Collecting stamps is Tom's hobby. He started collecting stamps when he was six years old. Today, Tom has over a thousand stamps in his collection.

    a. Tom collects stamp albums.

    b. Tom started collecting stamps in high school.

    c. Tom is a stamp collector.

    d. Collecting stamps is an expensive hobby.

13. Mother went to market. She bought apples, oranges, and bananas. She also bought cabbage, beans, and squash.

    a. Vegetables in the market are expensive.

    b. Mother bought chicken and meat.

    c. Many people went to the market.

    d. Mother bought fruits and vegetables.

14. Tommy and Timmy are brothers. They look the same. They also have the same birthdays.

    a. Tommy is older than Timmy.

    b. Timmy is more handsome than Tommy.

    c. Tommy and Timmy are twins.

    d. Tommy and Timmy are best friends.

15. Girls love roses. They smell so sweet. Their colors are also very attractive.

    a. Roses are fragrant.

    b. Roses attract bees.

    c. Boys love roses.

    d. Girls don't like roses.

16. For this question, use your knowledge of the real relations between the existing nouns to determine the best response.

LUKO is colder than ice
SUKO is warmer than steam
GRAKO is colder than ice

Which of the following is correct?

    a. LUKO is the coldest
    b. GRAKO is warmer than LUKO
    c. SUKO is the warmest
    d. GRAKO is colder than LUKO

17. For this question, use your knowledge of the real relations between the existing nouns to determine the best response.

SANCHO is taller than PANCHO
KEMCHO is shorter than molehill
SANCHO is taller than mountain

Which of the following is correct?

    a. PANCHO is taller than mountain
    b. KEMCHO is the shortest
    c. SANCHO is the tallest
    d. KEMCHO and PANCHO are of same height

18. For this question, use your knowledge of the real relations between the existing nouns to determine the best response.

LIMO is faster than tortoise
SUMO is of same speed as cheetah
KUOMO is faster than LIMO

Which of the following is correct?

    a. Tortoise is the slowest
    b. KUOMO is faster than SUMO
    c. Cheetah is the fastest
    d. None of the above

19. For this question, use your knowledge of the real relations between the existing nouns to determine the best response.

LULU is lighter than KUKU
BUBU is denser than lead
KUKU is as light as paper

Which of the following is correct?

    a. KUKU is denser than lead
    b. LULU is not the lightest
    c. BUBU is the densest
    d. None of the above

20. For this question, use your knowledge of the real relations between the existing nouns to determine the best response.

LONU is as sweet as sugar
BANU is spicier than chili
NONU is sweeter than chili

Which of the following is correct?

    a. NONU is the sweetest

    b. LONU and sugar are the sweetest

    c. BANU is not the spiciest

    d. None of the above

21. For this question, you must reverse the real relation between the existing nouns to determine the best response.

A SOMA resembles a MAMA but is smaller
A GAMA resembles a worm but is bigger
A MAMA resembles an elephant but is smaller

Which of the following is correct?

    a. MAMA is bigger than worm

    b. Elephant is smaller than SOMA

    c. Worm is bigger than GAMA

    d. MAMA is smaller than GAMA

22. For this question, you must reverse the real relation between the existing nouns to determine the best response.

A SASA is stronger than chalk
A MUXA is weaker than gold
A LALA is weaker than MUXA

Which of the following is correct?

    a. SASA is not the strongest

    b. MUXA is weaker than chalk

    c. LALA is not the weakest

    d. None of the above

23. For this question, you must reverse the real relation between the existing nouns to determine the best response.

A TAGO resembles an ant but is heavier
A LAGO resembles an elephant but is lighter
A ROGO resembles a TAGO but is heavier

Which of the following is correct?

    a. TAGO weighs less than an elephant

    b. LAGO weighs as much as ROGO

    c. ROGO is the heaviest

    d. None of the above

24. For this question, you must reverse the real relation between the existing nouns to determine the best response.

KAKA is thicker than water
SUKA is of same thickness as blood
BUKA is thinner than blood

Which of the following is correct?

    a. SUKA is the thinnest

    b. BUKA is thicker than water

    c. water is thicker than SUKA

    d. KAKA is not the thickest

25. For this question, you must reverse the real relation between the existing nouns to determine the best response.

AON is longer than worm
BAON is smaller than snake
SAON is longer than BAON

Which of the following is correct?

    a. BAON is the smallest

    b. AON is the longest

    c. SAON is the longest

    d. SAON is smaller than nano

26. For this question, you must reverse the real relation between the existing nouns to determine the best response.

JIJA is colder than Africa
SUJA is warmer than Antarctica
GUJA is colder than Africa

Which of the following is correct?

    a. JIJA is the coldest

    b. GUJA is warmer than JIJA

    c. SUJA is the warmest

    d. GUJA is colder than JIJA

27. For this question, you must reverse the real relation between the existing nouns to determine the best response.

AIRA is taller than GAIRA
BAIRA is shorter than Mt. Everest
AIRA is taller than dwarf

Which of the following is correct?

    a. GAIRA is taller than dwarf

    b. BAIRA is the shortest

    c. AIRA is the tallest

    d. BAIRA and GAIRA are of same height

28. For this question, you must reverse the real relation between the existing nouns to determine the best response.

MOLI is faster than car
SULI is of same speed as cycle
KULI is faster than MOLI

Which of the following is correct?

    a. Car is the slowest

    b. KULI is faster than SULI

    c. Cycle is the fastest

    d. None of the above

29. For this question, you must reverse the real relation between the existing nouns to determine the best response.

GAGA is lighter than SASA
RARA is denser than cotton
SASA is as light as iron

Which of the following is correct?

    a. SASA is denser than cotton

    b. GAGA is not the lightest

    c. RARA is the densest

    d. None of the above

30. For this question, you must reverse the real relation between the existing nouns to determine the best response.

BRAVO is as sweet as pepper
AAVO is spicier than jaggery
NAVO is sweeter than jaggery

Which of the following is correct?

    a. NAVO is the sweetest

    b. BRAVO and pepper are the sweetest

    c. AAVO is not the spiciest

    d. None of the above

Situational Judgement

Scenario 1

An editor complains about your work regardless of how much you try. How should you deal with a difficult supervisor?

    a. Ignore his negative comments and stay positive

    b. Listen attentively to the criticism and try to comply.

    c. Refer to the company's policy document for further information.

    d. Blame the supervisor for being ignorant.

Scenario 2

Workload is increasingly becoming a problem in your department. How should you work to improve the situation?

   a. Assign more work to a junior employees as well as divide the work more efficiently.

   b. Request more staff or temporary help from the management.

   c. Ask for higher pay for you and your team.

   d. Do what you can and leave what you can't.

Scenario 3

Your team goes out for a party but there is a line-up and the wait time is too long. Some of your team grow impatient and want to leave. How should you handle this situation?

   a. Offer incentives and ask them to be patient.

   b. Request patience for a little while longer.

   c. Lead them in demonstrating against the unfair treatment.

   d. Keep quiet and let things fall into place.

Scenario 4

Suppose you fail while undertaking a project given to you by your supervisor. How should you react?

   a. Freak out and blame the failure on yourself and your team.

   b. Ensure that you learn from the mistakes and move on.

   c. Ignore the failure and console yourself that failure is inevitable.

   d. None of the above.

Scenario 5

You have been given an assignment together with a colleague. During the time when you need crucial information, your colleague takes too long time to respond. What should you do?

    a. Discuss with your colleague and see if there is a solution.

    b. Discuss the matter with your immediate supervisor.

    c. Demand that he keeps you posted at all times and respond faster.

    d. Acquire information from other sources on your own.

Scenario 6

The company you work for undergoes various changes. You, and some of the employees, are finding it hard to adjust to rapid and constant changes. How should you act in such a situation?

    a. Rebel against the proposed changes.

    b. Read new company books to improve yourself.

    c. Mobilize other employees to attend training.

    d. Become more actively involved in the changes.

Scenario 7

As a team leader, your company assigns you with a huge project. What are the first steps you should take?

    a. Explain the project and goals to everyone.

    b. Involve only the people you deem important to avoid confusion.

    c. Ask for assistance from the experienced supervisors.

    d. Decline any assistance from anybody who may deter your project.

Scenario 8

You are in charge of a team that looks up to you for many things not just on work related issues. You learn some very bad news which needs to be delivered to your team. How should you go about it?

    a. Be straight forward and direct.

    b. Avoid addressing issues that could be unwelcome to the team.

    c. Bring them together and explain as much as possible. Address their concerns.

    d. Ask someone else to deliver the bad news on your behalf.

Scenario 9

You notice that your team members are actively competing against each other on a project you are overseeing. How should you react?

    a. Discourage any sort of competition.

    b. Monitor the competition to ensure that it's healthy and productive towards achieving the goals.

    c. Allow unregulated competition where the smartest wins.

    d. Offer a reward for the most productive.

Scenario 10

You face a lot of criticism at work for something you did. This weighs you down and affects your general performance. What should you do?

    a. Find areas to criticize those criticizing you.

    b. Let the matter be addressed by your supervisors.

    c. Resent the critic.

    d. Work on improving the aspect criticized by my colleagues.

Scenario 11

After working on a project for several months, it becomes clear to you that reorganizing the team is inevitable in realizing the project's vision. What should you do?

    a. Discard the current team and form another.

    b. Match the strengths of the team members with the overall goals stipulated.

    c. Remove the less skilled employees and replace them with more experienced ones.

    d. Do nothing.

Scenario 12

Some of the junior employees in your company are not under your jurisdiction yet their co-operation is important for the success of your business. How should you handle the situation?

    a. Demand for cooperation from them.

    b. Call them to a meeting and stress on the fact that you are a boss and they need to cooperate.

    c. Clearly communicate your ideas and be open to feedback.

    d. Request their supervisors to order them to cooperate with your department.

Scenario 13

You are the manger in given line of production. John, a junior employee, disregards your orders. How should you handle the situation?

    a. Request that the employee is fired immediately.

    b. Set an example by disciplining the rogue employee.

    c. Hear out and understand the reason for his disagreement.

    d. Change the directive.

Scenario 14

New facts come to your attention mid-way through a project. They require you to change most or all of your plan. How do you go about changing the decisions already made?

    a. Always keep clear communication between and among the members of the team.

    b. Abruptly change the initial plan.

    c. Consult with others on what needs to be done.

    d. Disregard the new facts.

Scenario 15

One of your employees disagrees with you concerning a new business plan. How do you go about formulating and presenting your argument without hurting them?

    a. Rebuke the employee for disobedience

    b. Over-rule the objections.

    c. Base your argument on objective facts and listen to their side of the argument.

    d. Call for disciplinary action against the employee.

Scenario 16

An agent has worked tirelessly with other company agents with no success. This client is then referred to you for assistance. How should you go about assisting the client?

    a. Refer the client to another agent who is more competent.

    b. Refuse to accept the client.

    c. Listen attentively to the issue troubling the client and offer professional assistance as you deem best.

    d. Attend to the client similar to how he has been attended in the past.

Scenario 17

The company you are working for has experienced communication hiccups and misunderstandings in the past. How should you prevent similar incidents in the future?

    a. Encourage all employees to use written communication.

    b. Make clarifications where needed and encourage team members to do the same.

    c. Refuse to consider any verbal communication.

    d. Be complacent in communicating with others.

Scenario 18

A workmate is very mean to you. You disregard this but the issue has recently been putting a lot pressure on you. You need to stay positive and motivated. How should you handle this?

    a. Become mean to them as well.

    b. Confront his ill behavior.

    c. Involve supervisors in resolving the conflict.

    d. Keep on motivating yourself to become better.

Scenario 19

A client walks into your office requesting assistance with a product. Since you are less involved in this area, you cannot help him. How should you handle the situation?

    a. Refer the client to the correct department.

    b. Welcome the client and be as hospitable as possible as you find the right person to assist him.

    c. Find the correct information and assist the client.

    d. Inform the client that the areas requested is outside your scope.

Scenario 20

A client you have been serving becomes impatience with the process. She goes out looking for the manager saying that you are taking too long to give her the assistance.

What should you do to diffuse the situation?

    a. Refuse to attend the client.

    b. Take this matter to your supervisor.

    c. Explain the process to the client why it is taking longer.

    d. Ignore the client completely.

Scenario 21

You work as a consultant in an audit firm with five co-workers in your team reporting to a team manager who reports to a department manager.

Matt, a co-worker you share an office with, requires your advice on a report he is about to present the weekly team meeting. Your team manager leads the meetings but the department manager is present usually.

Although the part of the report Matt shows you looks fine, you observe missing conclusions of the numerical analysis of a different section of the report. This does not meet the required standards of your departmental supervisor.

Matt looks confident about the part of the report and does not seem interested in your opinion.

What should you do?

    a. There is not much you can do if he is not interested in your opinion. You let it go and let him face the consequences of presenting an incomplete report.

    b. Notify the management if he is not keen on listening to you. Talk to your manager and let him explain to Matt why the changes are necessary.

c. Put in the necessary effort to make him listen. This may be a little uncomfortable, but you explain the reasons behind your criticism hoping Matt will understand.

d. Try to educate him by showing him proper reports and company policy.

Scenario 22

You are working as a management trainee in a leisure company and are currently placed at a busy leisure club in the city center. You get a call from head office that a small leisure club has an abnormally large number of staff on off due to sickness today. You are requested by head office to spend time at that leisure club as the manager is off and his deputy is on holiday. However, you have a pile of paperwork and several meetings with your team at your club.

What should you do?

a. Explain your situation and inquire from the head office contact how you are supposed to prioritize your day.

b. Suggest that you are given 30 minutes to reschedule your day and promise to give them a response after half an hour.

c. Since you are busy suggest that they call other nearby clubs to find a manager who might be able to step in to help the understaffed club.

d. Agree to spend time at the understaffed club but take your paperwork with you.

Scenario 23

You have been a graduate trainee with the government for close to six months. You joined the program with 3 trainees that you have been working with closely on several projects. You notice one of your colleagues has not been usual for a while.

You also over-hear your manager say she was not impressed by his contribution during a customer meeting. You and this colleague are supposed to jointly deliver work for a customer the following week. You think he will not be able to deliver successfully.

What should you do?

    a. Take him for coffee and ask him how he is doing and express your concern that you are worried he has not been himself lately.

    b. Take him aside and explain to him that you can tell he is not functioning to his level best and offer to take up majority of the work on the following weeks project.

    c. Monitor him closely for a while, and intentionally find ways to work with him more closely.

    d. Approach your manager and let him know that you overheard him talk about your colleague. Let him know that you also think there are some problems.

Question 24

You hold a position as a graduate trainee position at a global bank branch. You have been requested by your manager to recommend options that will increase opportunities for business development within the branch. Several initiatives have been put in place to offers\ solutions for small businesses with little success. The team has been trained on the solutions and other branches have had success marketing them in their areas. The team in your branch is responsible for selling these packages with individual targets in place.

What should you do?

a. Talk to colleagues in branches that have been more successful and ask them what they are doing to be successful in their efforts to sale these packages.

b. Run another short training about the packages to the branch members responsible for selling them to customers.

c. Suggest that you come up with a free networking event for local businesses one evening at a nearby hotel.

d. Suggest you can call several local businesses to discuss the offer and try to close some sales personally.

Scenario 25

You noticed there is a lot of useful research conducted for clients while working as a graduate trainee for a consulting firm. You can see that clients and colleagues would benefit from this but there is no clear method to disseminate this. You discuss it the manager and suggest ways to make the practice even better.

What should you do?

a. Propose that you have a webinar every 90 days where key players in the company share findings from their research with others.

b. Suggest a two-day internal conference every year that focusses on sharing research findings among employees.

c. Suggest an area is created on the company internal network where employees are encouraged to share what they discover from their research.

d. Suggest the company sets up a research forum with the purpose of ensuring the research findings are shared in the company with departmental representatives from all departments.

Scenario 26

You work as a trainee in a large bank. An upset client calls while you are working in the customer service department. He claims he has not received a refund on some fees he was charged in error. He claims one of your colleagues promised the money would be in his account today but has not yet arrived. He is getting upset and is raising his voice.

What would you say?

> a. "If you give me your account details, I will do all I can to investigate what happened."
>
> b. "Let me talk to the colleague you mentioned to get to the bottom of this. Please hold on a couple of minutes I will talk to him and get back to you."
>
> c. "I understand that you are upset but please calm down so that I can help you."
>
> d. "I believe there is a good reason for this. Give your account details so I can investigate."

Scenario 27

You are working in an electronics company as a trainee and are part of an international project looking at new marketing opportunities. You find it difficult to understand what a colleague is saying during a conference call. She is also a graduate trainee and during your interactions on other calls you have got on well. She has a strong accent and speaks very quickly when she is nervous. You are in the meeting room with several colleagues and the project lead. You can see that your colleagues are also having a difficult time understanding her.

What should you do?

a. When she is no longer speaking, send her a private message explaining to her that she should slow down a little as several people are finding it difficult to understand her.

b. Discuss your concerns after the call to other team members and suggest you compare notes to ensure you are on the same page.

c. Mention your concerns to the project lead after the call and offer to talk to your colleague since you have a working relationship.

d. Call your colleague after the call and ask how she finds the project. Politely mention that you find it difficult to understand what she says at times and suggest that slowing down would help.

Scenario 28

You submitted a paper to an upcoming professional global conference. You have attended the conference before and have met people from your industry and universities around the world. The paper has a summary of a research you conducted and believe it will be helpful. You learned that the paper has been accepted and you have been asked by your manager to find a way to present the paper that will make the biggest impact. You have limited time for your presentation.

How do you respond?

a. Say you will employ the use of graphics and images to draw out key messages.

b. Say you will create a presentation that reflects the research with similar section headers.

c. Ask the manager what they think would be the best approach from their experience.

d. Say that you will take time introducing the research approach but take most of the time talking about your findings and conclusions.

Scenario 29

You operate a 10-person group. You have professional and cooperative workers. However, you have recently found that they are taking longer breaks and work generally has been declining. You are pleased that the workplace has a nice environment, yet you are concerned with its effect on the jobs of your team.

How should you respond?

> a. Announce that any employee wanting to take a break must first ask you about that.
>
> b. Announce that only one worker should have a coffee break at any specified moment.
>
> c. Speak to the staff regarding the situation and ask for cooperation.
>
> d. Warn team members with the deadlines and suggest there will be consequences.

Scenario 30

You feel some changes are needed after reading a study prepared by one of your team. When discussing the study with her, she disagrees with several of your statements and feels it is a stronger report at present.

What are you going to do?

> a. Explain why your opinion more thoroughly.
>
> b. Let her realize that your choices are final, but display empathy to her effort.
>
> c. Tell her it is her job, and you value her view. Your feedback will support her, and she will be able to approve or deny it.
>
> d. Politely invite her to object to and clarify your remarks.

Scenario 31

You are asked to prepare a presentation for your staff, with the help of your co-worker, Daniel. Your boss will make the presentation to the board of directors for approval. Daniel manages the data collection department. He is tasked with collecting data while you convert the data into PowerPoint slides. Daniel has gathered data from a paper that was incorrect - this has led you to create 30 misleading slides.

On the day you have the briefing, the supervisor counts on you to have everything ready with a lot more to do.

What is the best way to respond?

a. Describe to the boss how Daniel gathered the data and why it took a long time. Ask Daniel if he can fix the error he made- much of it was his own.

b. Let the boss know that you and Daniel got the data incorrect while putting together the presentation. Modify the introduction slides.

c. Do not call attention to this error. Give him handwritten notes during class with corrections to use while presenting.

d. Do not annoy the boss about this anymore. You can notify Daniel right away about changing the faulty slides.

Scenario 32

Bob is new to the office staff. Your superior, has assigned you to teach Bob the computer system due to your experience. It is a relatively simple system, however, Bob is finding it difficult to understand.

What should you do?

a. Tell him it should be easy for everyone to understand and he needs to learn it quickly.

b. Allow Anna, who has more experience than you, to conduct the lesson. Return to your other activities for the rest of the day.

c. Tell Bob to do it later. You become irritable and have to complete other tasks.

d. Discuss with Bob the issues he is having with the system. Start a new training session at a much simpler level.

Scenario 33

A client calls and criticizes you for not delivering a product by the deadline. You lookup the order and see the delivery is late due to a shortage.

What should you tell the client?

a. "I apologize; your order is delayed due to a shortage. Would you like me call when it is dispatched? "

b. "I am afraid we seem to be out of stock at the moment, but I'm certain your package will be delivered soon."

c. "The shipment has not yet been shipped; you are correct. We are out of stock right now, but I cannot do anything about that."

d. "I am afraid; this commodity seems to be out of stock now. For a while, you'll have to be careful."

Scenario 34

The store has just received a new brand of cell phone. Before marketing this new phone, which of the following is the most critical as a sales representative?

    a. Ensure the new phone is appropriately displayed in the shop.

    b. Estimate the new product's impact on thew market.

    c. Review how competitors portray the new phone.

    d. Test the commodity yourself and get acquainted with it.

Scenario 35

You work in department that shares office space with others. Everyone in your department is given a new computer system and you are left out.

What should you do?

    a. Consider this as a small mistake and talk to the head of department.

    b. Confront the head of department and ask him to explain why you are being treated unfairly.

    c. Take a new computer from a colleague.

    d. Make a complaint with the HR department.

Scenario 36

You have the knowledge that company property has been going missing for some time now. You noticed a colleague putting small things from the office in her handbag several times and suspect she is responsible.

What should you do?

> a. Find ways to get more evidence or catch her in the act.
>
> b. Face your colleague and ask her about what you have noticed then inform your manager of your suspicion.
>
> c. Raise the issue in a meeting and mention that you suspect your colleague.
>
> d. Don't do anything. Your colleague will be caught if she is guilty.

Scenario 37

After a busy day at work, you send an email with confidential information to a client by mistake.

What should you do?

> a. Leave the office and handle the matter the following day.
>
> b. Overlook the mistake, re-send the email to the correct address.
>
> c. Immediately contact the wrong recipient via phone or email to explain the mistake. Then send the email to the right person.
>
> d. Explain to your manager what happened and let them handle the matter.

Scenario 38

A patient suffering from a complex medical condition dies after a long period of treatment. Although there is enough evidence to fill a death certificate, your consultant is keen on taking a postmortem to investigate the death. The family consents to his request. However, the family speaks to you and claims they were coerced into making the decision and not happy.

What should you do?

    a. Send the family back to the consultant and ask him to speak to them again.

    b. Talk to your consultants and find out his reasons for the postmortem.

    c. Request another senior colleague to meet with the family and discuss their concerns.

    d. Personally, talk to the family about their concerns.

Scenario 39

Which action should be avoided when listening to an upset customer describing a problem?

    a. Listen carefully to the customer describing the problem.

    b. Politely requesting the customer to calm down that you can offer your assistance.

    c. Directing the customer to your supervisor.

    d. Putting effort on focusing the customer to their original need.

Scenario 40

You walk into the washroom and find a colleague crying. What should you do?

    a. Walk out and give them peace.

    b. Find the manager and leave the situation to them.

    c. Ask whether they are fine and if there is anything you can do to help.

    d. Give them a hug at tell them everything will be okay.

SEQUENCES

1. Consider the following sequence: 64, 50, 38, 28, 20, ... Find the first three terms.

    a. 15, 10, 5
    b. 14, 10, 8
    c. 10, 0, -10
    d. 12, 4, -6

2. 2 4 8 16 | 5 10 20 40 | 4 8 16 32 | 3 6 ... 24

    a. 4
    b. 12
    c. 8
    d. 10

3. Consider the following sequence: 23, ..., 31, 37. What is the missing number?

    a. 19
    b. 27
    c. 29
    d. 30

4. Consider the following sequence: 6, 8, 4, 10, 18, 22, ...
What number should come next?

   a. 34
   b. 32
   c. 24
   d. 26

5. Consider the following sequence: 10, 13, 16, 19, ...
What 3 numbers should come next?

   a. 21, 23, 25
   b. 21, 24, 27
   c. 22, 25, 28
   d. 23, 26, 29

6. Consider the following sequence: 17, 23, 29, 35, ...
What 3 numbers should come next?

   a. 41, 47, 54
   b. 42, 47, 53
   c. 40, 45, 50
   d. 41, 47, 53

7. Consider Box A and the relationship to the numbers in Box B. What is the missing number in Box B?

Box A

8	12
5	9

Box B

19	27
13	?

   a. 18
   b. 21
   c. 24
   d. 14

8. Consider the following sequence:
8, 11, 9, 12, 10, 13, ... What number should come next?

   a. 11
   b. 10
   c. 15
   d. 16

9. Consider the following sequence:
2, 1, (1/2), (1/4), ... What number should come next?

   a. 1/3
   b. 1/8
   c. 1/16
   d. 2/8

10. Consider the following sequence: 10, 20, 40, 80, ... What number should come next?

   a. 150
   b. 120
   c. 90
   d. 160

11. Consider the following sequence: 18395, 18295, 18195, 18095, ... What number should come next?

   a. 18000
   b. 18950
   c. 17995
   d. 17905

12. Consider the following sequence: -45, -39, -33, -27, ... What number should come next?

   a. 21
   b. -21
   c. -25
   d. 25

13. Consider the following sequence: -100, 100, -200, 0, -300 ... What number should come next?

   a. 0
   b. -200
   c. -100
   d. 100

14. Consider the following sequence:
2.3, 2.3, 4.6, 12.18 ... What number should come next?

   a. 24.36
   b. 48.72
   c. 48
   d. 12.19

15. Consider the following sequence:
3, 9, 11, 33, 36, ... What number should come next?

   a. 106
   b. 39
   c. 33
   d. 108

16. Consider the following sequence:
345, 347, 344, 346, ... What number should come next?

   a. 345
   b. 343
   c. 348
   d. 349

17. Consider the following sequence:
21, 21, 31, 31, 41, 41, ... What number should come next?

   a. 51
   b. 50
   c. 61
   d. 31

18. Consider the following sequence: 12, 19, 29, 42, ... What number comes next?

   a. 56
   b. 55
   c. 58
   d. 57

19. Consider the following sequence: 3.5, 5, 7, 4, 14, 3, 28, 2, ... What number comes next?

   a. 60
   b. 56
   c. 48
   d. 1

20. Consider the following sequence: 2, 5, 11, 23, 47, ... What number comes next?

   a. 56
   b. 95
   c. 77
   d. 85

Problem Solving

1. A woman spent 15% of her income on an item and ends with $120. What percentage of her income is left?

   a. 12%
   b. 85%
   c. 75%
   d. 95%

2. A mother is making spaghetti for her son. The recipe that she's using says that for 500 grams of spaghetti, she should add 0.75 grams of salt. However, the mom just wants 125 grams of spaghetti. Based on this information, how much salt should she use?

    a. 0.38 grams
    b. 0.75 grams
    c. 0.19 grams
    d. 0.25 grams

3. A pet store sold $19,304.56 worth of merchandise in June. If the cost of products sold was $5,284.34, employees were paid $8,384.76, and rent was $2,920.00, how much profit did the store make in June?

    a. $5,635.46
    b. $2,714.46
    c. $14,020.22
    d. $10,019.80

4. At the beginning of 2009, Madalyn invested $5,000 in a savings account. The account pays 4% interest per year. At the end of the year, after the interest was awarded, how much did Madalyn have in the account?

    a. $5,200
    b. $5,020
    c. $5,110
    d. $7,000

5. If 144 students need to go on a trip and the buses each carry 36 students, how many buses are needed?

    a. 6
    b. 5
    c. 4
    d. 3

6. If a square if five feet tall, what is its area?

    a. 5 square feet
    b. 10 square feet
    c. 20 square feet
    d. 25 square feet

7. John is a barber and receives 40% of the amount paid by each of his customers. John gets all tips paid to him. If a man pays $8.50 for a haircut and pays a tip of $1.30, how much money goes to John?

    a. $3.92
    b. $4.70
    c. $5.30
    d. $6.40

8. Susan was surprised to find she had two more quarters than she believed she had in her purse. If quarters are the only coins, and the total is $8.75, how many quarters did she think she had?

    a. 35
    b. 29
    c. 31
    d. 33

9. There were some oranges in a basket, by adding 8/5 of these, the total became 130. How many oranges were in the basket?

    a. 60
    b. 50
    c. 40
    d. 35

10. Mr. Brown bought 5 burgers, 3 drinks, 4 fries for his family and a cookie for the dog. If the price of all single items is same, at $1.30 and a 3.5% tax is added, then what is the total cost of dinner?

   a. $16.00
   b. $16.90
   c. $17.00
   d. $17.50

11. A distributor purchased 550 kilograms of potatoes for $165. He distributed these at a rate of $6.4 per 20 kilograms to 15 shops, $3.4 per 10 kilograms to 12 shops and the remainder at $1.8 per 5 kilograms. If his total distribution cost is $10, what will his profit be?

   a. $10.40
   b. $8.60
   c. $14.90
   d. $23.40

12. The price of a book went up from $20 to $25. What percent did the price increase?

   a. 5%
   b. 10%
   c. 20%
   d. 25%

13. The price of a book decreased from $25 to $20. What percent did the price decrease?

   a. 5%
   b. 10%
   c. 20%
   d. 25%

14. A motorcycle travels at 50 km/hour for 25 minutes. How far does it travel?

    a. 10 km
    b. 20.83 km
    c. 25 km
    d. 22.85 km

15. A woman spends 3/5 of her salary on rent, and 1/6 on utilities and saves the rest. How much will she save in 1 year?

    a. 2 2/5 monthly salary
    b. 2 months salary
    c. 2 1/5 monthly salary
    c. 1 4/5 monthly salary

Answer Key

Logic & Analytical Reasoning

1. A
True

2. B
False - Although all students carry a backpack, not everyone who carries a backpack is a student.   i.e. there are some people who carry a backpack who are not students.

3. B
False – Just because all dogs are mammals does not mean that all mammals are dogs.

4. B
False – Based on the first 2 statements you could say that all felines are mammals, but you cannot say that all mammals are felines.

5. B
False

6. B
False

7. B
False – you cannot reach a negative conclusion from 2 positive statements

8. C
The only certain thing is Krizzia and Nea are related to each other.

9. A
The only certain thing is the villagers rely on fishing to earn money since they live near the ocean.

10. C
The only certain thing is Ben and Ted are inseparable.

11. B
The only certain thing is Karen is fond of gardening.

12. C
The only certain thing is Tom is a stamp collector.

13. D
The only certain thing is mother bought fruits and vegetables.

14. C
The only certain thing is they are twins.

15. A
The only certain thing is roses are fragrant.

16. C
Based on real relations, ice is colder than steam. From first & third statements, LUKO and GRAKO are both colder than ice. From second statement, Suko is warmer than steam which is warmer than ice. Ice is warmer than both LUKO and GRAKO. Therefore, SUKO is the warmest. Relationship between LUKO and GRAKO can't be established.

17. C
Based on real relations, mountain is taller than a molehill. From second statement, KEMCHO is shorter than molehill which is shorter than mountain. From third statement, SANCHO is taller than mountain, which is taller than molehill and KEMCHO. From First statement, PANCHO is shorter than SANCHO, which makes SANCHO the tallest. The relationship of PANCHO with others isn't clear.

18. A
Based on real relations, tortoise is slower than cheetah. Based on first statement, LIMO is faster than tortoise. Based on second statement, SUMO and cheetah are of same speed and therefore, faster than tortoise. Based on third statement, KUOMO is faster than LIMO and therefore faster than tortoise. Therefore tortoise is slower than everybody and therefore tortoise is the slowest. Second and third choices are inconclusive.

19. C
Based on real relations, paper is lighter than a cheetah. Based on second statement, BUBU is denser than lead. Based on third statement, KUKU and paper are of same density and therefore, lighter than BUBU. Based on first statement, LULU is lighter than KUKU and therefore lighter than BUBU. Therefore BUBU is denser than everybody.

20. D
Based on real relations, sugar is sweeter than chili. Based on second statement, BANU is spicier than chili. Based on first statement, LONU and sugar are of same sweetness and therefore, sweeter than BANU. Based on third statement, NONU is sweeter than chili and therefore sweeter than BANU. Therefore BANU is the spiciest. But it's not clear whether NONU is sweeter than LONU and sugar or not. Therefore we can't conclude anything on who is the sweetest.

21. D
Based on the relations outlined in the second statement, we know that a GAMA is bigger than a worm, which, on reversing real relations between worm and Elephant as mentioned in the question, is bigger than an Elephant. From third statement, we know that the elephant is bigger than MAMA. We know that SOMA is smaller than MAMA from first statement. From smallest to biggest, the order of the words is: SOMA, MAMA, Elephant, Worm, GAMA. Therefore, choice D is correct.

22. B
Based on reversing real relations, chalk is stronger than gold. From the first statement, we know SASA is stronger than chalk which is stronger than gold. From second statement, we know that MUXA is weaker than gold, and therefore weaker than chalk and SASA. From third statement, we know that LALA is weaker than MUXA and therefore weaker than other three as well. From weakest to strongest, the order of the words is: LALA, MUXA, gold, chalk, SASA.

[LALA<MUXA<gold<chalk<SASA in STRENGTH]

23. C
If we reverse real relations, an ant is heavier than an elephant. From first statement, we see that TAGO is heavier than ant which is heavier than an elephant. From third statement, we know that ROGO is heavier than TAGO (and therefore heaviest) while, from second statement, we know that LAGO is lighter than elephant (and therefore lightest). From lightest to heaviest, the order of the words is LAGO, elephant, ant, TAGO, ROGO.

[ROGO>TAGO>ant>elephant>LAGO in weight]

24. C
If we reverse real relations, water is thicker than blood. From first and second statements, KAKA is thicker than water, which is thicker than blood, which is of same thickness as SUKA. From third statement, BUKA is thinner than blood and therefore the lightest. From heaviest to thinnest, the order of the words is KAKA, water, blood & SUKA, BUKA.

[KAKA>water>blood=SUKA>BUKA]

25. A
Reversing real relations, worm is longer than a snake. From first statement, AON is longer than worm ,which is longer than snake. From second statement, snake is longer than BAON. From third statement, SAON is longer than BAON, making BAON the smallest. Relationship between SAON and AON is unclear.

Therefore, choice A is correct. The other choices are inconclusive.

26. C
Reversing real relations, Africa is colder than Antarctica. From first & third statements, JIJA and GUJA are both colder than Africa. From second statement, SUJA is warmer than Antarctica which is warmer than Africa. Africa is warmer than both JIJA and GUJA. Therefore SUJA is the warmest. Relationship between JIJA and GUJA can't be established.

27. C
Reversing real relations, dwarf is taller than Mt. Everest. From second statement, BAIRA is shorter than Mt. Everest which is shorter than dwarf. From third statement, AIRA is taller than dwarf, which is taller than Mt. Everest and BAIRA. From First statement, GAIRA is shorter than AIRA, which makes AIRA the tallest. The relationship of GAIRA with others isn't clear.

28. A
Reversing real relations, car is slower than cycle. Based on first statement, MOLI is faster than car. Based on second statement, SULI and cycle are of same speed and therefore, faster than car. Based on third statement, KULI is faster than MOLI and therefore faster than car. Therefore car is slower than everybody and therefore car is the slowest. The second and third choices are inconclusive.

29. C
Reversing real relations, iron is lighter than cotton. Based on second statement, RARA is denser than cotton. Based on third statement, SASA and iron are of same density and therefore, lighter than RARA. Based on first statement, GAGA is lighter than SASA and therefore lighter than RARA. Therefore RARA is denser than everybody.

30. A
Reversing real relations, pepper is sweeter than jaggery. Based on second statement, AAVO is spicier than jaggery. Based on first statement, BRAVO and pepper are of same sweetness and therefore, sweeter than AAVO. Based on third statement, NAVO is sweeter than jaggery and therefore sweeter than AAVO. Therefore, AAVO is the spiciest. But it's not clear whether NAVO is sweeter than BRAVO and pepper or not. Therefore, we can't conclude anything on who is the sweetest.

SITUATIONAL JUDGEMENT

1. B
The editor is your boss and that's the way things are so if they are not happy that will mean some adjustment on your part. However, if you feel the editor is being unreasonable, you may want to talk with them. Choice C, referring to the company policy document is a possibility depending on the situation.

Choice A, ignorance is no defense in any situation in life. By ignoring to address the concerns of the clients you set a pace for failure. You are bound to lose more clients. Choice D, blaming the supervisor will only lead to more complications. Building resentment and bad publicity are sure consequences of such behavior.

2. A
Division of labor and specialization are the best ways of solving increasing workload. This gives the employees equal time to work on given tasks to ease the workload. Division of labor pro-motes innovation and invention and increases output per employee.

Choice B, may be a good idea, however management very likely has limited options to help. Choice C, asking for higher pay doesn't solve the problem. Choice D, may be a good option if, and only if all else fails.

3. B
You are nominally in charge so it fall on you to handle the situation. However, you can't do much about the line-up. Choice B, ask for patience for a bit longer is the best choice. Choice A, offering incentives may be considered later depending on how long you wait. Choice C, and D don't do anything to diffuse the situation.

4. B
Life is sequence of lessons that start from childhood and continues in adulthood. By learning from one's mistake, you are likely to improve next time. Sometimes we succeed and sometimes we learn. Failure is a part of life and we all should embrace failure as a lesson for a better tomorrow. It may

be necessary to discuss the failure and learnings with your supervisor.

Choices A, C and D do not addresses the core issue.

5. A

First, discuss it with your colleague. There may be things you are not aware of preventing them from getting information to you quickly. If this doesn't work, go to the other options.

Choice B, going to your supervisor is an option for later. Choice C, is not a great approach. Making demands is not likely to change anything. Choice D, getting information from other sources would mean that there is a disharmony between the key participants. This may be an option for later or as a last resort.

6. D

The changes are going to continue so your choice is to resist (difficult) or become more involved. Once you are more involved in why the changes are taking place they become easier to manage.

7. A

Making sure everyone understands the goals of the project gets everyone on board is the first step.

Choice B, discriminating against team members will alienate them. Asking for assistance, choice B, from others is a necessity but comes after being clear on goals and obtaining feedback. Choice D, declining assistance is not a good strategy to start.

8. A

A straightforward and direct approach is best. Sugar coating or avoiding the bad news will come back on you.

Choices B and C, avoiding the issue and blaming others will cause problems later. Choice C, getting others to related bad news will also cause problems later.

9. B
The aspect of monitoring carries the weight in this scenario. Unregulated competition could lead to unethical behaviors. Competition is healthy in any business and human encounters. By regulating the competition, the goals are likely to be met easily.

Choice A, discouraging competition loses the benefits of competition. Competition is healthy provided limits are defined and observed. Choice D, is a good choice but choice A is better. Offering a reward may come later.

10. D
Self-improvement is a continuous process and any person who can't handle feedback or criticism positively loses the opportunity to improve.

Choice A and C, retaliating against your critics or resenting, is destructive. You can't win an argument and even when you think you have, the resentment stirred in your victim works against you and your plans. Choice B, giving the matter to supervisors, may be a next step but not a good strategy initially.

11. B
Finding and correctly matching the strengths of the individual team members with those needed in the business is the most appropriate course of action. Performance analysis will assist you in determining which employee fits which position and assigning them duties in those areas.

Choices A and B, discarding or replacing members of the team and replacing would be time consuming.

12. C
Clear communication is vital in such a scenario as a first step. If this doesn't resolve the issue the other choices are next steps.

Incorrect answers B and D
Being bossy (choice B) leads to resentment. Choice D, requesting their supervisor intervene is a possible next step.

13. C
Unless you are able to understand the reason behind the disagreement, you will not be in a position to accomplish much. By taking time to break down the details of the disagreement the chances of reaching a consensus are higher.

Terminating the employee (choice A) does not benefit the company. Choice B, disciplining is an option for later. Choice D suggests for a complete overhaul of the initial plan.

14. A
Team members need clear communication to assimilating the changes. This approach ensures that none of the team members are left behind and everyone participates mapping out the changes.

New information is to be considered and deliberated on to avoid misunderstandings. Abruptly changing or disregarding the facts will not succeed (Choices B and D). Choice C, consulting others may be necessary as a next stop.

15. C
Be objective in finding a common ground with the employee. Base your argument on facts and consider both sides of the story. Don't make accusations.

Choices A, B and D, over-ruling, rebuking or disciplining may be necessary but not as a first step.

16. C
Listening is the key to assist the client. This way you have a chance of understanding the concerns raised by the client. You will also be in a better position to close a sale.

Choice A, referring the client to another agent, you have lost the client and possibly their friends and relatives. You reduce their level of confidence in you and your company. Choice D, repeating what has been happening is also not likely to be of help to the client. Choice B, refusing the client may be an option if the issues are too difficult, but not as a first step.

17. A
Verbal communication is not always the best because there is never proof of communication. The best way to communicate is through written communication. By following written communication, you are provided with evidence of communication for reference in future.

Choice B, refusing to consider verbal communication is too extreme. Choice D is incorrect be-cause you don't want to be complacent when communicating with others.

18. C
Some of the disagreements require input from higher authority. Supervisors are in a better position to resolve a conflict between junior employees.

Choice A is not a resolution. Choice B, confronting the behavior may work if done properly, but could also make the situation worse, however, choice C is the better choice. Choice D, motivating yourself could work towards making you feel better but not towards resolving the conflict.

19. B
Choice B is the best choice. Being hospitable and polite is key.

Directing the client to other unknown offices could confuse him and you miss an opportunity. Choice C, finding the right information may seem a good choice, however, the client should be referred to an expert and knowledgeable person.

20. C
Clear communication is the best choice.
Choice B, taking this matter to the authority may make a person appear incompetent and unable to handle simple situations. Choice D is incorrect since customer satisfaction should always be a top concern.

21. A
You have tried to help, and that is the best that you can do. Choice B, notifying the management seems excessive at this point. Choice D, trying to educate him is using up your time and effort, and since he doesn't seem receptive, probably a waster of time.

22. A
As an employee you are supposed to be flexible and be ready to help when needed. As much the management trainee is held up by other responsibilities explaining the situation to head office might help as his meetings can be rescheduled and the deadlines on the paperwork extended.

23. A
Talking to him will let him know that people care about him. He might be able to open up and talk about the challenges he is facing. Venting might help him relax and focus on his work better. Remember you aren't a counsellor but a friend and co-worker and this is a casual conversation.

24. A
Speaking to colleagues of other branches that have been successful is the best solution. Learning from the successful branches will save you wasted energy and time. Other choices, such as choice C, a networking event, or choice D, calling customers personally are good second steps.

25. D
Choice D gives the company a continuous way of sharing research findings. Creating a research forum will give employees a chance to discuss all matters research as much as they want in the forum. Having people from different departments will mean they can be able to share ideas and expertise constantly.

26. A
By choosing response A the client will be assured that their issue will be taken care of. This response makes no superficial promises, and no blame is shifted to the bank or the other colleague.

27. D
Calling her after the call will enable you maximize on the good relationship you already have and she will probably be more receptive. Politely mentioning that you find it difficult to understand her will be helpful as she might not be aware that her accent affects, her communication and slowing down will be a good solution provided. This choice does not es-

calate the situation as discussing with other team member (choice B) as well as the project lead (choice C).

28. C
The manager, from their experience, will have ideas on the best way to present the material with the greatest impact. Asking for his guidance will enable you tap into his experience and make an impactful presentation.

29. C
Your workers' self-discipline is lacking and is presently harming their performance. You understand your team's good qualities and want to protect it but are still anxious about the potential of your team. Team members are friendly and have demonstrated particularly good success in the past, so appealing to their collaboration is most likely to produce results. This direct contact demonstrates the capacity to efficiently connect and control workers and to effectively use methods to improve efficiency. This approach aims to promote employee growth and development.

Introducing targets and pushing them may be a feasible tactic. It is a good form of rising efficiency. Nevertheless, this reaction often involves a punitive measure, which is too early to pursue.

30. D
Response D will be the one that encourages a genuine debate. This answer gives you more details, and you can consider together with your employee in a clear exchange of views (decision making - taking staff input). This reply demonstrates that you value the viewpoint of your staff while respecting and retaining your own opinion. It is the safest option. Different situations require different approaches to authority - in some roles; you must be stern.

In contrast, in others, an approach to instructional oversight is favored (as a guide). Choice D is the best option because it indicates that you care about your subordinates' input in the decision-making phase.

31. B
Selecting choice B, demonstrates responsibility and accep-

tance of the effects of one's actions. Daniel was more responsible than you for making the mistake. However, by sharing that responsibility with your teammate, you show that you are a team player (teamwork). Suppose you let your boss know that you have made a mistake. In that case, you are showing that you are responsible and have the integrity of admitting your mistakes – thus allowing your boss to be considerate of the possibility of being late for the deadline.

When you and your team work together to add an amendment to the document organically, it allows you to perfect your submission on time.

Choice A may sound like the right solution because Daniel is responsible for the issue. However, you are not prepared to divide the guilt, so you are dropping all the burden on Daniel and not offering to work together on fixing the issue. Besides, you can unintentionally harm his reputation with the boss by attacking Daniel behind his back— as he should be offered a chance to clarify.

32. A
It is the only approach when you search for the root of Bob's issues. Understanding what he finds challenging, you are showing strong listening skills. You often demonstrate adaptability by adjusting the solution to the issue. By being supportive and providing answers, you are a team player to improve the understanding of your colleague.

It might be more beneficial to let another worker with more expertise take over. However, your boss has assigned you this assignment, and it is not your duty to assign it to anyone else. Most likely, the issue does not rely on the degree of expertise but the method of teaching. You do not demonstrate the adaptability of your method of teaching by letting Anna teach him.

33. A
This answer is clear and direct.
Choice A starts by apologizing. The response given in this reply option adds an invitation to contact the customer, giving additional service and explaining operation and service guidance.

Choice C understands the customer's concern but has no constructive effort ("I cannot do anything"), giving the appearance you are not accountable for the issue.

34. D
This question assesses how you navigate the transition to marketing a new product (adaptability). The most important approach is to familiarize yourself with the product by checking it yourself (choice D). As a sales agent, you need to be comfortable when showing it to customers.

In choices A, B, and C
It is necessary to ensure that the product display is attractive and appropriate (choice A) but not critical. It is interesting to read the product's success (choice B), which may help with your sales, but not critical. It is important and may be useful, to see what competitors are doing, (choice C) but also not critical.

35. A
Choice A is the best response. If you have not been given the right tools and equipment to do your job, talking to your head of department or direct supervisor is the right move. It is the responsibility of your head of department to help ensure you have all it takes to do your job.

Jumping to conclusions that you have been treated unfairly or taking a new colleague's computer may prove embarrassing if it was a simple mistake.

36. B
This is the right thing to do as it will give you the chance to discuss the matter with your colleague first and clear ambiguity. It is also your responsibility to report the matter to your manager.

37. C
This is the right thing to do. Explaining the mistake to the client will help protect the integrity of the message then send the email to the right person.
This is assuming the contents of the email is not catastrophic! Otherwise choice D may be appropriate.

38. B
As a professional you need to find out more about why your colleague insists on having the postmortem before anything else. This will help when talking to the family as you will be able to provide professional counsel. Your partner may have genuine concerns that need to be addressed.

39. A
Choice B should be avoided because by asking the customer to calm down instead of helping them to do so you are indirectly telling them they lack self-control. You will sound impatient and rude. Choice C, referring to the supervisor may give the customer the impression of giving them the run-around.

40. C
Response C is appropriate as shows that you have empathy. Even if you are not able to help the colleague will feel more relieved as a problem shared is a problem half solved.

SEQUENCES

1. B
Each number is minus 2 from the previous.

2. B
Each number in the sequence is double the last number.

3. C
The numbers are consecutive primes (divisible only by 1 and themselves)

4. B
Each number is the sum of the previous and the number 2 places to the left.

5. B
This sequence is increasing by adding 3 to each term.

6. D
Each element in the sequence increases by 6.

7. B
The numbers in Box B are the result of (number in Box A * 2)+ 3. So the missing number is 21.

8. A
The sequence increases initially and then decreases in the next term. The relationship between each increase is +3 and the relationship with the alternate decrease is -3. So the answer is -2 from the last given term. 13 – 2 = 11.

9. B
The sequence is decreasing by half. So half of 1/4 = 1/8

10. D
The sequence is increasing. Each new term is obtained by multiplying the last term by 2. Therefore, 80 x 2 = 160

11. C
Each new term is calculated by subtracting 100 from the last term. So, 18095 – 100 = 17995

12. B
Each new term is calculated by adding 6 to the last term, therefore, -27 + 6 = -21

13. C
The sequence increases initially and then decreases in the next term. The relationship between each increase is +200 and the relationship with the alternate decrease is -300. So the answer is -300 + 200 = -100

14. B
Each new term is derived by multiplying the last term with an increasing number. The first term is multiplied with 1 to get the next term. That is multiplied with 2 to get the 3rd term, which is multiplied with 3 to get the 4th term. So the answer is 12.18 x 4 = 48.72

15. D
The sequence increases by multiplying by 3 and adding 3. The first term the sequence is increasing by multiplying and adding 3 alternatively. The first term was multiplied by 3 to get the second term, and that was added to 3. The answer = 36 x 3 = 108

16. B
The sequence increases and decreases alternatively. The rate of increase is +2 and decrease is -3, so answer = 346 – 3 = 343

17. A
The sequence is increasing after repeating the last term. The answer = 41 + 10 = 51

18. C
The second term increased by 7 and subsequent terms increased by adding 3 to the last rate of increase. The last given term increased by +13 to get 42. The next term will be 42 + 13 + 3 = 58

19. B
The sequence is increasing and decreasing. The 1st term doubles to get the 3rd term, which doubles to get the 5th term and that doubles to get the 7th term and so on. The 2nd terms decreases by 1 to get the 4th terms, which decreases by one to get the 6th term and so on. The answer is the 7th term 28 x 2 to get the 9th term= 56.

20. B
The second term increased by 3 and subsequent terms increased at twice the rate of last increase. The last given term 47 increased by 24, the next term will be 47 + 48 = 95

PROBLEM SOLVING

1. B
Spent 15% - 100% - 15% = 85%

2. C
125 : 500 is the same as 25 : 100 or 1 : 4. So the amount of salt will be 0.75/4 = 0.1875, or about .19 grams.

3. B
Total expenses = 5284.34 + $8,384.76 + $2,920.00 = $16,589.10

Profit = revenue less expenses

$19,304.56 - 16589.10 = $2,715.46

4. A
$5,000 at 4% = 5000 X 4/100
5000 X .4 = 200
So the total after one year will be $5,200

5. C
If each bus carries 36 students, and there are 144 students total, then 144/36 = 4 buses.

6. D
If a square is 5 feet tall, then the area will be 5 X 5 = 25.

7. B
John's total will be 40% of 8.50 plus the tip of $1.30.

8.5 X 4/100 = 8.5 X .4 = 3.40

Total = 3.40 + 1.30 = $4.70.

8. D
If she has $8.75, that will equal 35 quarters. ($8.00 = 32 quarters and $.75 = 3 quarters, total 35 quarters).

She had 2 more quarters than she thought, so she had 35 - 2 = 33 quarters.

9. B
Suppose oranges in the basket before = x, Then: X + 8x/5 = 130, 5x + 8x = 650, so X = 50.

10. D
As price of all the single items is same and there are 13 total items. So the total cost will be 13 × 1.3 = $16.90. After 3.5 percent tax this amount will become 16.9×1.035=$17.50.

11. B
The distribution is at three different rates and amounts:

$6.4 per 20 kilograms to 15 shops ... 20•15 = 300 kilograms distributed

$3.4 per 10 kilograms to 12 shops ... 10•12 = 120 kilograms distributed

550 - (300 + 120) = 550 - 420 = 130 kilograms left. This amount is distributed by 5 kilogram portions. So, this means that there are 130/5 = 26 shops.

$1.8 per 130 kilograms.

We need to find the amount he earned overall these distributions.

$6.4 per 20 kilograms : 6.4 * 15 = $96 for 300 kilograms

$3.4 per 10 kilograms : 3.4 * 12 = $40.8 for 120 kilograms

$1.8 per 5 kilograms : 1.8 * 26 = $46.8 for 130 kilograms

So, he earned 96 + 40.8 + 46.8 = $ 183.6

The total cost of distribution is given as $10

The profit is found by: Money earned - money spent ... It is important to remember that he bought 550 kilograms of potatoes for $165 at the beginning:

Profit = 183.6 - 10 - 165 = $8.60

12. D
The price increased by $5 ($25-$20). The percent increase is 5/20 x 100 = 5 x 5=25%

13. C
The price decreased by $5 ($25-$20). The percent increase = 5/25 x 100 = 5 x 4 =20%.

14. B
50 km/hour is 50/60 per minute = 0.8333 km/hour, so in 25 minutes it will travel 25 * 0.8333 = 20.83 km.

15. A
Setup the equation - 3/5 + 1/6 + X = 1
Find a common denominator 18/30 + 5/30 + X = 1
23/30 + X = 1
X = 1 - 23/30
X = 7/30 (amount of monthly savings)
so in 1 year she will save 12 X 7/30 = 84/30
= 2 12/30 = 2 2/5

PRACTICE TEST QUESTIONS SET 2

The questions below are not the same as you will find on the PSEE - that would be too easy! And nobody knows what the questions will be and they change all the time. Below are general questions that cover the same subject areas as the PSEE. So, while the format and exact wording of the questions may differ slightly, and change from year to year, if you can answer the questions below, you will have no problem with the PSEE.

For the best results, take these practice test questions as if it were the real exam. Set aside time when you will not be disturbed, and a location that is quiet and free of distractions. Read the instructions carefully, read each question carefully, and answer to the best of your ability.

Use the bubble answer sheets provided. When you have completed the Practice Questions, check your answer against the Answer Key and read the explanation provided.

Do not attempt more than one set of practice test questions in one day. After completing the first practice test, wait two or three days before attempting the second set of questions.

Logic and Analytical Reasoning

	A	B	C	D	E		A	B	C	D	E
1	○	○	○	○	○	21	○	○	○	○	○
2	○	○	○	○	○	22	○	○	○	○	○
3	○	○	○	○	○	23	○	○	○	○	○
4	○	○	○	○	○	24	○	○	○	○	○
5	○	○	○	○	○	25	○	○	○	○	○
6	○	○	○	○	○	26	○	○	○	○	○
7	○	○	○	○	○	27	○	○	○	○	○
8	○	○	○	○	○	28	○	○	○	○	○
9	○	○	○	○	○	29	○	○	○	○	○
10	○	○	○	○	○	30	○	○	○	○	○
11	○	○	○	○	○						
12	○	○	○	○	○						
13	○	○	○	○	○						
14	○	○	○	○	○						
15	○	○	○	○	○						
16	○	○	○	○	○						
17	○	○	○	○	○						
18	○	○	○	○	○						
19	○	○	○	○	○						
20	○	○	○	○	○						

Situational Judgement

	A	B	C	D	E		A	B	C	D	E
1	○	○	○	○	○	21	○	○	○	○	○
2	○	○	○	○	○	22	○	○	○	○	○
3	○	○	○	○	○	23	○	○	○	○	○
4	○	○	○	○	○	24	○	○	○	○	○
5	○	○	○	○	○	25	○	○	○	○	○
6	○	○	○	○	○	26	○	○	○	○	○
7	○	○	○	○	○	27	○	○	○	○	○
8	○	○	○	○	○	28	○	○	○	○	○
9	○	○	○	○	○	29	○	○	○	○	○
10	○	○	○	○	○	30	○	○	○	○	○
11	○	○	○	○	○	31	○	○	○	○	○
12	○	○	○	○	○	32	○	○	○	○	○
13	○	○	○	○	○	33	○	○	○	○	○
14	○	○	○	○	○	34	○	○	○	○	○
15	○	○	○	○	○	35	○	○	○	○	○
16	○	○	○	○	○	36	○	○	○	○	○
17	○	○	○	○	○	37	○	○	○	○	○
18	○	○	○	○	○	38	○	○	○	○	○
19	○	○	○	○	○	39	○	○	○	○	○
20	○	○	○	○	○	40	○	○	○	○	○

Sequences

	A	B	C	D
1	○	○	○	○
2	○	○	○	○
3	○	○	○	○
4	○	○	○	○
5	○	○	○	○
6	○	○	○	○
7	○	○	○	○
8	○	○	○	○
9	○	○	○	○
10	○	○	○	○
11	○	○	○	○
12	○	○	○	○
13	○	○	○	○
14	○	○	○	○
15	○	○	○	○
16	○	○	○	○
17	○	○	○	○
18	○	○	○	○
19	○	○	○	○
20	○	○	○	○

Problem Solving

	A	B	C	D
1	○	○	○	○
2	○	○	○	○
3	○	○	○	○
4	○	○	○	○
5	○	○	○	○
6	○	○	○	○
7	○	○	○	○
8	○	○	○	○
9	○	○	○	○
10	○	○	○	○
11	○	○	○	○
12	○	○	○	○
13	○	○	○	○
14	○	○	○	○
15	○	○	○	○

LOGIC AND ANALYTICAL REASONING

1.
All colonels are officers.
All officers are soldiers.
No colonels are soldiers.

If the first 2 statements are true, then the third statement is:

   a. True
   b. False
   c. Uncertain

2.
No houses on Appleby Street or Francisco streets cost more than $500,000. My house is not on Appleby or Francisco Street.

My house does not cost more than $500,000.

If the first 2 statements are true, then the third statement is:

   a. True
   b. False
   c. Uncertain

3.
Some tropical fish are very sensitive.
I have many types of tropical fish. Some of my fish are very sensitive.

If the first 2 statements are true, then the third statement is:

   a. True
   b. False
   c. Uncertain

4.
Most people in oil producing countries are rich.

I live in an oil producing country.
I am rich.

If the first 2 statements are true, then the third statement is:

    a. True
    b. False
    c. Uncertain

5.
Science can explain all events. Making a decision is an event. Science cannot explain how I make a decision.

If the first 2 statements are true, then the third statement is:

    a. True
    b. False
    c. Uncertain

6.
Doctors can sometimes predict epidemics.

Bird Flu is becoming an epidemic. Doctors know where bird flu will spread.

If the first 2 statements are true, then the third statement is:

    a. True
    b. False
    c. Uncertain

7.
That store sells new and used books.
My textbook is used.
My textbook came from that store.

If the first 2 statements are true, then the third statement is:

    a. True

    b. False

    c. Uncertain

8. Angel gets the highest grades in all the subjects in school. She is also the president of the student body. Every year she gets the highest award given by the school.

    a. Angel is a slow learner.

    b. Everybody admires Angel.

    c. Other children are envious of Angel.

    d. Angel is at the top of her class.

9. John is fond of the color green. He always wears green shirts to school. His rubber shoes are also green. His bag, raincoat, and notebooks are also green

    a. John has green eyes.

    b. John hates the color green.

    c. John like the color green.

    d. John wears blue rubber shoes to school.

10. The Earth is the only planet with known life forms. It is the third planet from the sun in the solar system. It rotates on its axis in 24 hours and revolves around the sun in 365 ¼ days.

    a. There is no life on Earth.

    b. The Earth is round.

    c. The Earth is the farthest planet in the solar system.

    d. Many living things live on Earth.

11. Rhea helps mother with the household chores everyday. She sweeps the floor every morning. She also helps mother prepare food for the family. She washes the dishes too.

    a. Rhea is helpful.

    b. Rhea is too lazy to do household chores.

    c. Rhea waters the plants.

    d. Rhea cooks for the whole family.

12. The children enjoy playing football after school. Sometimes, they play basketball with other kids. On weekends, they play baseball, badminton, or tennis.

    a. Children prefer playing indoors.

    b. Children enjoy different kinds of sports.

    c. Children hate playing.

    d. Playing is a form of exercise.

13. Jane spends her free time reading. She likes to read books, magazines, and even newspapers. She reads stories about adventures and fairy tales.

    a. Jane likes to watch television.

    b. Jane spends her free time writing stories.

    c. Jane's hobby is reading.

    d. Jane reads stories in school.

14. The body is made up of many bones. The skull protects the head. The ribs protect the chest. There are also small bones that protect the ears.

    a. Bones are connected to the muscles.

    b. Bones are present in the stomach.

    c. Animals have bones.

    d. Bones protect different parts of the body.

15. Trees give off oxygen. They also provide shade during sunny days. Some trees bear fruits while others are used to build houses.

    a. Trees have many purposes.
    b. Trees aren't important to men.
    c. Birds build nests in trees.
    d. Roots and trunk are parts of a tree.

Situational Judgement

Scenario 1

Daniel is working on a project that seems to give him a lot of difficulty. He has shown signs of depression in the last week.

What should you do to help him out?

    a. Motivate Daniel trying to get the bottom of his issues.
    b. Inform the supervisors.
    c. Take him for some counseling sessions.
    d. Do absolutely nothing.

Scenario 2

A sales seminar you attended insists that to close more sales, you need to work on making a better first impression.

What should you do to close more sales?

    a. Dress smartly and speak clearly.
    b. Conduct business as usual.
    c. Dramatize your ideas to create rapport.
    d. Ignore the advice from the supervisor.

Scenario 3

You are working with a cross-functional team. The other team members are not keen about the recommendations you give. You are worried they may sacrifice quality to the point of jeopardizing customer privacy.

What would you do?

> a. Pick concrete issues where you feel that the project is at risk and bring them to your manager.
>
> b. Insist on a plan to minimize the risks you have seen.
>
> c. State your concerns and let the team decide on the way forward.
>
> d. Write a memo to the team on the potential risks so the in case of a problem you can deflect the blame.

Scenario 4

As an employee of many years at your company, you feel totally demotivated and dissatisfied with your work. You need to improve.

What are you likely to do to achieve your objectives?

> a. Find a new place to work.
>
> b. Find new tasks to re-engage your interest.
>
> c. Listen to motivational speeches.
>
> d. Learn to always stay positive.

Scenario 5

Some of your team members are less committed than in the recent past.

How should you go about improving commitment?

    a. Introduce work incentives.

    b. Reduce compensation for the employees who are not producing.

    c. Talk to the employees on the need of being committed.

    d. Fire the team and get another team.

Scenario 6

Sam, a 30 year-old employee in your organization has shown exemplary work. You want to praise his work in front of the other employees.

How should you go about praising him?

    a. Wait until everyone is together and compliment him.

    b. Contrast his work with the poor work of the others.

    c. Email all the employees.

    d. Ignore this idea.

Scenario 7

While working with your team members on a project you realize that things are not going well.

How should you motivate the team to perform better?

    a. Meet regularly to discuss on issues.

    b. Explain how lucky they are.

    c. Select the best team players and assign them more responsibility.

    d. Become actively involved in daily operations of the business.

Scenario 8

Most of the strategies you have adopted thus far don't seem to be working in getting team to do the right thing. You feel the need to set an example.

How should you go about this?

    a. Work twice as hard.

    b. Report to work early and leave late.

    c. Lecture the team to strive to be like you.

    d. Condemn the team for being lazy.

Scenario 9

You have formulated the goals of your department together with your team members. However, you realize that you are not yet sure on how those goals are going to be achieved.

How should you go about such a situation?

    a. Read and re-read the goals for full comprehension.

    b. Ensure team members understand what is required of them.

    c. Brainstorm on ideas that could get you to your goal.

    d. Just do the work anyhow.

Scenario 10

You are in a fast-paced environment and your job demands that you achieve a set objectives. This, according to you is a real challenge.

How should you achieve your objectives?

    a. Let the team know the deadlines to the set objectives.

    b. Keep the information to yourself.

    c. Work three times harder.

    d. Use the internet to learn more.

Scenario 11

While communicating with your juniors and superiors, you realize that several things are hindering you from staying actively engaged in the conversation.

How would you address this issue?

    a. Start practicing yoga and wellness meditation.
    b. Be keen and attentive while communicating.
    c. Listen attentively without thinking.
    d. Do not judge.

Scenario 12

You and your team encounter new challenges on a certain project. You realize the need to rally the team behind the project to get through this difficult time.

How should you achieve this?

    a. Show the team that you value their input.
    b. Be harsh to the team members.
    c. Assert your authority as a supervisor.
    d. Dictate what needs to be done during hard times.

Scenario 13

You have been assigned a new type of project. None of you are qualified to undertake the project.

How should you handle this situation?

    a. Let the team know the deadlines to the set objectives.
    b. Keep the information to yourself.
    c. Call a meeting and strategize.
    d. Use the internet to learn more.

Scenario 15

After realizing losses for some time now, your supervisor blames you and your team. However, you know for sure that it was the supervisor who is responsible for the loss.

How should you handle the situation?

    a. Blame the loss on the supervisor.

    b. Take up this matter to higher authority.

    c. Explain to the team that you are being blamed and strategize.

    d. Deny the blame.

Scenario 16

You overhear discussions during coffee break about your planned termination. However, you feel that you are being wrongfully accused.

How would you react in such a situation?

    a. Explain your side of the story.

    b. Accuse other employees.

    c. Blame the company.

    d. Accept defeat and go home.

Scenario 17

You are required to collaborate with a coworker who is tough to please. For the success of the project, both of you need to work together. What is the first step dealing with this situation?

    a. Stay calm and try to understand their point of view.

    b. Demean them and disregard their input.

    c. Report to your supervisor that you can't work with them.

    d. Ignore their unhelpful behavior.

Scenario 18

Your colleague has recently been criticized for poor performance. You need to do something to uplift their spirits.

How should you go about this?
    a. Criticize his weaknesses.

    b. Tell of his critics.

    c. Show that you care.

    d. Encourage them to learn from their mistakes.

Scenario 19

You are an employee at a company that has adopted new technology, and everyone feels uncertain and out of place. How would you go about making them feel comfortable and more productive?

    a. Introduce more training.

    b. Give them positive feedback.

    c. Rebel against the new technology.

    d. Ensure that everyone feels involved in the company.

Scenario 20

In the past, your department has been commended for excellent performance. You notice one of your team members is distracted, distressed and falling behind.

How would you address this issue?
    a. Refer him to the guidance and counseling team.

    b. Actively listen to his problems and compare them with yours.

    c. Report this matter to your supervisor.

    d. Actively listen and advise him to the best of your ability.

Scenario 21

During your morning brief, the Infection Control instructs that all staff must roll up their sleeves when having clinical interactions with patients. During your shift, your colleague has her sleeves down.

What should you do?

> a. Tell Infection Control that your colleague is not complying with their policy
>
> b. Speak directly to your colleague about your observation.
>
> c. Raise your observation with to the nurse in charge of the ward.
>
> d. Do not say anything immediately but monitor the situation over the course of the next few days

Scenario 22

A patient with end-stage respiratory failure that requires continuous oxygen therapy informs you that he knows he is dying and wants to die at home. He has not talked about this to anyone as he thinks it will upset his family and the nurses taking care of him.

What should you do?

> a. Tell him that he needs to stay in hospital while on oxygen.
>
> b. Tell him that the team will take account of his wishes.
>
> c. Discuss with his family his wish to die at home.
>
> d. Discuss his home circumstances with his General Practitioner.

Scenario 23

A customer calls to raise a complain that a package he had ordered had not arrived by the due date. You check the order and find it had not been delivered as the product is out of stock.

What would you say?

a. "I apologize; we have a delay on your order. Would you like me to call you when we it has been dispatched?"

b. "I'm sorry, we seem to be out of stock, but I assure you the product will be delivered soon."

c. "You are right; the package has not been delivered because we are out of stock. There is nothing I can do to help."

d. "I'm sorry; we are currently out of stock of this product. You will have to be patient a little longer."

Scenario 24

A new mobile phone model has been stocked in your shop.

Which of these is the most important this you should do as a sales representative before selling this new model?

a. Ensure the product is displayed in the store prominently.

b. Research on the popularity of the new model.

c. Find out how the product is being presented by your competitors

d. Try out the product personally to familiarize with it.

Scenario 25

You have a colleague that keeps asking you to check their assignment at the last minute. The colleague has asked you to help edit her assignment when you are working on a presentation. You see that this will consume the better part of your day as it needs a lot of work.

What should you do?

a. Help with editing the document and find time to finish your presentation at night

b. Inform the colleague that you have no time and focus on your task

c. Let your manager know that your colleague's presentation is terrible and that you have no time to help

d. Help the colleague this time and plan a meeting to talk about this and find a way to handle such situations in the future.

Scenario 26

Your team been working on a project for months and it is almost complete. Your team will present your work to the client in a week. You discover an error in the modeling that could change the conclusion drawn. Correcting the analysis means you will have to redo all the work but there is no time for this.

What should you do?

a. Since no one noticed the error for such a long time ignore the error and make the presentation as it is.

b. Report it to your senior and find out what can be done.

c. Ask the most trusted team members to go through the material and discus what should be done.

d. Call the client and invent an excuse to get an extension.

Scenario 27

You are a supervisor where one of your juniors is a close friend to your manager and talks to the manager about your projects before you get a chance to report. This embarrasses you as he exaggerates the potential risks.

What should you do?

    a. Befriend the employee and establish better ground rules

    b. Ask your boss to only share information with you

    c. Maneuver the employee into difficult situations that cause poor performance and fire them

    d. Isolate this employee so they have less impact on your team

Scenario 28

You are working in as a retail assistant and discover a customer has been browsing your section for a while and is visibly getting frustrated. After talking to him you discover the item, he is looking for is not available. You have to inform him the Item is out of stock.

What should you do?

    a. Apologize that the item is out of stock and recommend an online retailer.

    b. Offer to order the item for the customer and promise to call him when the item arrives.

    c. Offer the customer the items serial number so that he can easily find it elsewhere.

    d. Suggests that he tries one of your other stores that is 40 minutes' drive away.

Scenario 29

You are working in a retail store with a colleague out on off. You discover that their section of the store is untidy while you are going on your tea break.

What should you do?

   a. Take your tea break and tidy it up on your way back if it remains the same

   b. Go back and ask for permission from your team leader to tidy up the place

   c. Do nothing as the team leader has it under control

   d. Inform the team leader that there is problem in his section

Scenario 30

You have been asked to increase your sale by 15% as compared to July last year. July is a difficult month for children book sales as parents don't buy books at the end of the term.

   a. Put a handwritten poster promoting your range of summer activity books for children.

   b. Pick up a selection of summer-themed books and summer activity books and put them at the front of the children's area

   c. Tidy up the children's book area.

   d. Approach as many customers as possible with children's books and showing them the wide range of summer children's books and their location.

Scenario 31

You are working on busy day and the credit card system suddenly fails. You are informed it will take the provider 15 minutes to fix the issue. There is a long queue of customers waiting.

What should you do?

>a. Inform the customers of the problem and the time it would take to solve the problem. This would save those paying by cash.
>
>b. Continue serving the customers and apologize for the absence of the credit card payment option.
>
>c. Ask the team leader what to do.
>
>d. Take your afternoon break and let the customer come back later.

Scenario 32

You have been concerned about increasing signs of poor team morale amongst your team.

What should you do?

>a. Summon the team leaders separately to hear their explanations
>
>b. Leave things to settle down for a while rather than causing anyone distress
>
>c. Approach some staff from each of the teams for an informal chat
>
>d. Hold a brainstorm meeting for all team leaders to get fresh ideas

Scenario 33

As graduate trainee manager, you have discovered that none of your team objectives have been achieved.

What should you do?

    a. Use 1-on-1's to discuss effective targets and to jointly agreeing new ones.

    b. Scrap the objective setting idea since it clearly doesn't work.

    c. Mail the team an urgent request to work more closely together.

    d. Organize a team meeting to discuss attitudes and lack of effort being shown.

Scenario 34

You are leading a daily huddle with your over-worked nursing team. A new, junior colleague has been regularly interrupting other team members as they voice their own problems. You think they're trying to impress their new team by monopolizing the medical answers to each problem raised.

What should you do?

    a. Tell the new nurse to stop distracting everyone from alternative solutions.

    b. Ask why your more experienced team members are not offering their own solutions.

    c. Firmly suggest to your new colleague that it's fairer to let everyone contribute.

    d. Assuming the others agree with you; state what you think is happening here.

Scenario 35

You manage a specialist customer service help desk and realize the team members are introverts and don't engage in a lot of conversations. This has led to poor team spirit and job satisfaction.

What should you do?

> a. Call a one-off emergency meeting to highlight objectives and the lack of collaboration.
>
> b. Start by introducing half-hour, weekly catch-up meetings for the team.
>
> c. Implement compulsory training courses on interpersonal skills as soon as possible.
>
> d. Familiarize yourself with the team objectives, then email regular updates on each one's progress.

Scenario 36

You have the responsibility to read through an intern's draft report and have discovered the report does not meet any of the objectives set. You have limited time to improve the report before presenting it to your client.

What should you do?

> a. Let your intern find out what happens when a client receives a sub-standard report.
>
> b. Forward the draft report to other analysts in your department for their own comments.
>
> c. Ask your own manager what would have happened if you hadn't checked this report.
>
> d. Email your collated amends to the intern; offering to explain each one in further detail.

Scenario 37

You are a busy team leader attending a meeting where the presenter has overrun the allocated time. You agree that the presentation is going on for too long.

What should you do?

    a. Leave the meeting and explain you have an urgent matter to attend to.

    b. Wrap up the session then set up a presentation review later.

    c. Wrap-up the session by secretly messaging the whole team to ask questions.

    d. Leave time management to the presenter as it is his/her responsibility.

Scenario 38

You work in a shared office next to a noisy colleague which is giving you a difficult time concentrating. No one is talking about it but you are not the only one inconvenienced.

What should you do?

    a. Refer the matter to your senior, since they have overall responsibility.

    b. Make even more noise than this colleague - to show them just annoying it is.

    c. Email your noisy colleague to complain, cc'ing in your manager.

    d. Talk to your noisy colleague and request more reasonable behavior.

Scenario 39

You are the team leader in your accounts department. The backlog of work cases increases by the day to the point that your colleagues are regularly missing weekly targets. You have to solve the issue before it escalates further.

What should you do?

a. Remind your team of the problems and the clear need to meet every deadline.

b. Communicate to your team that you are resolving the problems personally.

c. Stay positive - and ask your immediate superior for additional resources.

d. Meet with the team to tell them what you believe is causing the problems.

Scenario 40

You are new to a large company that uses software for supervision. Trying to cheat the software is a very serious crime that failing to report a colleague that cheats the system can land you in trouble. You discover 3 colleagues trying to cheat the system.

What should you do?

a. Immediately report the three colleagues.

b. Wait to see if they are good employees. Report them if they are lazy.

c. Report them if they are absent on Friday.

d. Look the other way as you have no evidence.

SEQUENCES

1. A D G   J M P   S V Y _____

    a. B N P
    b. O L M
    c. M P S
    d. B E F

2. ααβΩΩμ   ββΩμμα   Ω_____

    a. αβΩμα
    b. μΩΩαβ
    c. Ωμααβ
    d. Ωββαμ

3. Consider the following sequence: 11, 15, 20, 26, ... What 3 numbers should come next?

    a. 31, 37, 42
    b. 33, 41, 50
    c. 32, 38, 46
    d. 36, 46, 56

4. αβαβμ   ΩπΩπ$ β∞β∞©   ¥_____

    a. π¥μ β
    b. μπ¥α
    c. π¥πα
    d. ¥β∞Ω

5. +-++-+   *÷**÷*   x=xx=   _____

    a. &*+#=×
    b. +==÷&&
    c. #!%#!$
    d. !#!!#!

6. S S S SS   S S SS SS   S SS SS SS   _____

    a. S SS   SSS SSS
    b. SS SS SS SS
    c. S SS SSS SSSS
    d. S SS SS S

7. Consider the following sequence: 1000, 992, 984, 976, … What 2 numbers should come next?

    a. 968, 961
    b. 967, 960
    c. 968, 960
    d. 970, 964

8. Consider the following sequence: 0.1, 0.3, 0.9, 2.7, … What 2 numbers should come next?

    a. -8.1, -24.3
    b. 8.1, 24.3
    c. 5.4, 10.8
    d. -5.4, -10.8

9. Consider the following sequence: 32, 16, 8, 4, ... What 3 numbers should come next?

   a. 2, 1, 0.5
   b. 2, 0, -2
   c. 0, -4, -8
   d. 2, 1, 0

10. Consider the following sequence: 3, ..., 9, 12, 15. What is the missing number?

    a. 4
    b. 7
    c. 6
    d. 5

11. Consider the following sequence: 13, ..., 31, 0, 49, 58. What 2 numbers are missing?

    a. 19, 29
    b. 23, 41
    c. 22, 40
    d. 16, 24

12. Consider the following sequence: 95, 90, ..., 80, 75. What is the missing number?

    a. 87
    b. 85
    c. 86
    d. 80

13. Consider the following sequence: ..., 75, 65, 70, 60, 65, 55, ... What 2 numbers are missing?

   a. 70, 35
   b. 65, 35
   c. 70, 60
   d. 65, 30

14. Consider the following sequence: 91, 85, ..., ..., 67, 61. What 2 numbers are missing?

   a. 81, 71
   b. 78, 72
   c. 80, 70
   d. 79, 73

15. Consider the following sequence: ..., ..., 120, 129, 138, 147. Find the first two terms.

   a. 102, 111
   b. 100, 110
   c. 102, 112
   d. 99, 111

16. Consider the following sequence: ..., 95, 88, 93, 86, 91, 0. What 2 numbers are missing?

   a. 88, 98
   b. 90, 98
   c. 100, 84
   d. 90, 84

17. Consider the following sequence: 76, 64, 54, 46, ..., 36, 34, ... What 2 numbers are missing?

   a. 40, 32
   b. 40, 34
   c. 42, 30
   d. 42, 32

18. Consider the following sequence: 3, 0, 12, 0, 48, 96. What 2 numbers are missing?

   a. 6, 36
   b. 6, 18
   c. 8, 16
   d. 6, 24

19. Consider the following sequence: 13, ..., 31, 0, 49, 58. What 2 numbers are missing?

   a. 19, 29
   b. 23, 41
   c. 22, 40
   d. 16, 24

20. Consider the following sequence: 3, 13, 22, 30, 37, ... What number comes next?

   a. 45
   b. 47
   c. 43
   d. 42

Problem Solving

1. Richard sold 12 shirts for total revenue of $336 at 8% profit. What is the purchase price of each shirt?

    a. $25.76
    b. $24.50
    c. $23.75
    d. $22.50

2. In a local election at polling station A, 945 voters cast their vote out of 1270 registered voters. At polling station B, 860 cast their vote out of 1050 registered voters and at station C, 1210 cast their vote out of 1440 registered voters. What was the total turnout including all three polling stations?

    a. 70%
    b. 74%
    c. 76%
    d. 80%

3. In a factory, the average salary of all employees is $125. The average salary of 10 managers is $300 and average salary of workers is $100. What is the total number of employees?

    a. 30
    b. 40
    c. 25
    d. 50

4. In a 30 minute test there are 40 problems. A student solved 28 problems in first 25 minutes. How many seconds should she give to each of the remaining problems?

   a. 20 seconds
   b. 23 seconds
   c. 25 seconds
   d. 27 seconds

5. The total cost of building a fence around a square field is $2000 at a rate of $5 per meter. What is the length of one side?

   a. 80 meters
   b. 100 meters
   c. 40 meters
   d. 320 meters

6. In a class of 83 students, 72 are present. What percent of student is absent? Provide answer up to two significant digits.

   a. 12
   b. 13
   c. 14
   d. 15

7. The price of a product was increased by 45%. If the initial cost of the product was $220, what is the new cost of the product?

   a. $230
   b. $300
   c. $319
   d. $245

8. A worker's weekly salary was increased by 30%. If his new salary is $150, what was his old salary?

    a. $120.00
    b. $99.15
    c. $109.00
    d. $115.40

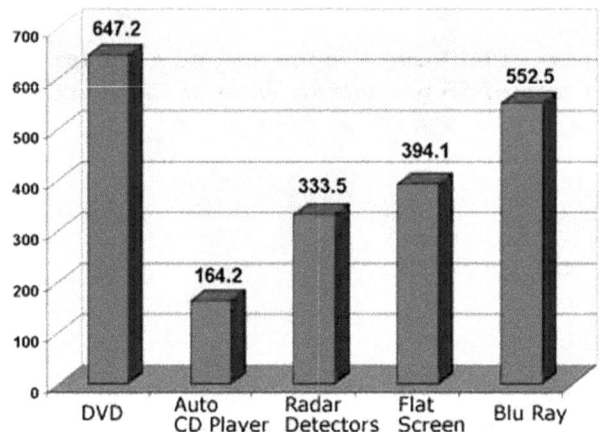

9. Consider the graph above. What is the third best-selling product?

    a. Radar Detectors
    b. Flat Screen TV
    c. Blu Ray
    d. Auto CD Players

10. Which two products are the closest in the number of sales?

    a. Blu Ray and Flat Screen TV
    b. Flat Screen TV and Radar Detectors
    c. Radar Detectors and Auto CD Players
    d. DVD players and Blu Ray

11. Great Britain has a Value Added Tax of 15%. A shop sells a camera for $545. If the VAT is included in the price, what is the actual cost of the camera?

   a. $490.40
   b. $473.90
   c. $505.00
   d. $503.15

12. The owner of a pet store decided to increase the cost of all reptiles 45%. If the initial cost of a reptile was $220, what is the new cost?

   a. $230
   b. $300
   c. $319
   d. $245

13. 5 men have to share a load weighing 10kg 550g equally among themselves. How much will each man have to carry?

   a. 900 g
   b. 1.5 kg
   c. 3 kg
   d. 2 kg 110 g

14. Peter drives 4 blocks to school and back every day. How many blocks does he drive in 5 days?

   a. 20
   b. 30
   c. 40
   d. 50

15. How much pay does Mr. Johnson receive if he gives half to his family, pays $250 for rent, and has exactly 3/7 of his pay left over?

    a. $3,600

    b. $2,800

    c. $1,750

    d. $3,500

Answer Key

Logic and Analytical Reasoning

1. False
Both premises to this argument use 'all,' so the conclusion (which uses 'no') must be false.

2. Uncertain
No information is given about houses NOT on Appleby or Francisco streets.

3. Uncertain
It is possible that some of my tropical fish are very sensitive, but it is also possible that they are all insensitive varieties.

4. Uncertain
I may be rich or I may not be.

5. False
IF Science can explain all events, AND making a decision is an event, THEN science CAN explain how I make a decision.

6. False.
There are 2 problems. Doctors can sometimes predict epidemics. Bird Flu is becoming an epidemic.

Bird flu is not an epidemic yet, and doctors can only predict epidemics sometimes.

7. Uncertain.
My textbook MAY have come from that store or it may have come from another store.

8. D
The only certain thing is Angel is at the top of her class.

9. C
The only certain thing is John likes color green.

10. D
The only certain thing is many living things live on Earth.

11. A
The only certain thing is Rhea is helpful.

12. C
The only certain thing is children enjoy different kinds of sports.

13. C
The only certain thing is Jane's hobby is reading.

14. D
The only certain thing is bones protect different parts of the body.

15. A
The only certain thing is trees have many purposes.

SITUATIONAL JUDGEMENT

1. A
By motivating him, you positively impact the results. Everyone needs a pat in the back and a person to motivate them when tough times comes.

Choice B, informing the supervisors, might not be the most appropriate thing to do, at least at first. As a colleague, its incorrect to do absolutely nothing (choice D). If motivating fails, you may then suggest counseling sessions (choice C).

2. A
The first impression is important in human encounters because it lasts through the duration the people get to interact. Good posture and clothing are indicators of success and the clients are likely to trust you more.

Choice C, dramatizing your idea does not necessarily mean that you create a good first impression. Choices B and D, ignoring the advice is no solution.

3. B
Insisting on a plan to minimize the potential risk will save the team from potential problems without involving anyone outside the team.

4. B

We all get bored easily by routine. By finding new tasks to engage, you trick the brain in staying active for longer periods of time.

Winners never quit, that is the basic principle in any form of business. As an employee, you shouldn't focus on getting a simpler job. Instead, your focus should be on building capacity to withstand and overcome challenges.

5. A

Introducing incentives is likely to motivate your team members. Choice B, reducing compensation is likely to alienating. Choice C, talking about the need to be committed could easily come across as talking down. Choice D, is not realistic.

While compensating the employees who perform exemplary, one creates unnecessary competition zones which could in turn be bad for business.

6. A

Complimenting him in public, you motivate other employees to do better. This is a sure way to increase their level of commitment to the success of the business.

Choice B, demeaning others will reduce moral and motivation. Choice C, emailing may be the only option under some circumstances but not the best.

7. A

Regular meetings keep everyone up-to-date to discuss issues, potential improvements and in touch with each other.

Choice B will not help. Choice C, selecting the best team players, means re-making the whole team – only as a last resort. Choice D, becoming more involved is good advice, but choice A is better.

8. B

If you want the best, you need to become the best. By working longer hours, you encourage your team members. Choice A is good, but choice B is better because it is more visible. Everyone will you arriving early and leaving late. Lecturing or condemning, choices C and D, never helps.

9. B
Making clear to the team the deadlines and what is expected of them is the first step.

Choice C is a good suggestion, if there is an issue with some parts of the project.

10. A
Making clear to the team the deadlines and what is expected and so everyone knows where they stand.

Choice B, keeping a monopoly of information is likely to cause chaos and lead to disruption. Working three times harder, choice C, however effective it may sound, is equally ineffective.

11. B
Communication is especially important in business environments. Being attentive while communicating you can avoid confusion and misinterpretation. Clear communication leads to better performance.

Although it sounds quite okay to practice yoga, choice A, not all employees understand what it is or the benefits and may not be interested.

12. A
Everybody wants to feel important. By ensuring that the employees feel involved, you keep morale and productivity up. Leadership styles vary greatly but the sure thing is being bossy to employees leads to reduced productivity. Asserting control or dictating makes people defensive and resist.

13. C
This is a challenging situation and getting everyone on board to solve is very important.

Choices A, B and D, are moving ahead blindly.

14. A
People buy things because they want the benefits. This is the only way to convince someone to buy.

The other choices, increasing pressure (hard-sell as choice B) ignoring objections, (choice C) don't work in the long term.

15. C
You are being blamed, and fair or not this is the reality. The first step is to strategize. Maybe this can be solved with a new strategy and maybe not.

Blaming the supervisor back doesn't solve the problem (choice A). Going over the supervisor's head, choice B, maybe a good strategy for your next step, but not initially.

16. A
It's important to make your side of the story known as a way to avoid confusion and misinterpretation.

By blaming and accusing others you don't help yourself.

17. A
The first step in dealing with difficult people is to stay calm and understand their point of view.

After that you can start to build rapport.

Choice C, reporting to your supervisor you can't work with them may be a second step but basically doesn't solve the problem. Choice D, ignoring their unhelpful behavior, depends on how serious it is – if it is minor this may be OK.

However, Choice A, is the best choice because you are going to have to get along with them.

18. D
The best thing with failure is the lessons it brings. By encouraging him or her to learn from their mistakes, you give them the chance to improve.

Choice A, criticizing does nothing to improving their situation. The person criticized will in turn find fault in you and blame you. Focus on the issues that bring success to the business.

19. D
Everyone wants to feel part of something and involved. As an employee your options are limited.

Training is great, (choice A) but as an employee you probably won't be able to. Rebelling, choice C, isn't going to change the situation.

20. A
It is important therefore to refer your colleague to a guidance session where he can get the appropriate assistance.

Comparing their problems with yours, Choice B, will not make them feel any better or be able to perform better. Reporting this matter to the supervisor, choice C, could solve the problem, but also could bring problems to your colleague and worsen their condition. Unless you have been trained on how to handle stress related issues, then it's not advisable to give counseling sessions to a person who shows signs of distress. It could accomplish quite the opposite.

21. B
This problem should be handled immediately and talking to your colleague addresses the urgency. This will also give the colleague a chance to change if what she did was genuinely by mistake.

22. D
Discussing the patient's home circumstances with his general practitioner before making any promises to him is the right thing to do. This will help you avoid giving false promises to the patient if his home circumstances are not conducive for his condition. The general practitioner will also advise on the right time to take him home.

23. B
Response B will be the right thing to say to the client. First you need to apologize for failing to deliver the package on time. Show integrity by giving the reason why the package has not been delivered without justification. The response also reassures the client that the package will be delivered.

24. D
Before selling a product, you need to have a feel of how the product works. This can only happen if you try out the product yourself. Familiarizing with the product will enable you understand how it operates and be able to address objections that might be raised by customers effectively.

25. D
Helping the colleague and finding a future remedy will save the current situation and provide a long-term solution.

26. B
Reporting the error to your senior is the right thing to do.

27. A
This will help the colleague understand the importance of respecting protocol.

28. B
Offering to go out of your way to ensure the customer gets what they wanted.

Choices A, C and D are incorrect. They do not address the issue in the most appropriate way.

29. B
Asking for permission is the right thing as you will be given ample time to tidy up.

30. D
Choice D is the best approach - a proactive approach.

31. A
Choice A is the best solution.

32. C
Talking to staff will help you uncover the root cause for the poor team morale.

33. A
Using 1-on-1's will open opportunities for each individual to work with their abilities.

34. B
Input from more experienced team members will solve the problem without sounding like you are shutting anyone down.

The other choices, A, C and D will make the junior colleague feel attacked.

35. B
Introducing a half-hour, weekly catch-up meeting will help people feel comfortable around each other and encourage conversations.

The other choices, A, C and D, are imposed solutions and will not be fully accepted.

36. D
This will help the intern know what to concentrate on in their future reports.

The other choices, A, B and C do offer long-term solutions.

37. B
this will save everyone's time as the entire team is paying little attention to the presentation.
The other choices, A, C and D do not provide solutions that will benefit the entire team.

38. A
Senior team members can handle the matter in the most appropriate manner.

The other choices, B, C and D may escalate the situation.

39. C
Requesting additional resources will go a long way in enabling your team work better.

Choices A, B and D will not solve the situation.

40. A
This is the right thing to do. Failing to report might also land you in trouble.

The other choices are all against the company policy.

Sequences

1. C
There are two letters missing in each sequence.

2. B
The sequence is decreasing. The first two terms decreased by 14 and subsequent differences is decreasing by 2, i.e. 14, 12, 10, 8, 6, 4, 2

3. B
The sequence is increasing by adding 4, 5, 6, 7, 8, 9....etc. The next term is of the sequence is 26 + 7 = 33 and then 33 + 8 = 41

4. C
The pattern alternates two figures and adds a new figure on the end.

5. D
The sequence alternates two instances, then one instance.

6. B
The sequences increases the double-digit 's' each instance.

7. C
The sequence is decreasing by 8.

8. B
The sequence is decreasing by dividing the last term by 2.

9. C
The sequence is increasing by half each time.

10. B
The sequence is increasing by multiplying the last term by 3. 2.7 x 3= 8.1 and 8.1 x 3 = 24.3

11. C
The sequence is increasing by 9.

12. B
The sequence is decreasing by 5.

13. C
The sequence is decreasing by +5 and -10 alternately. The first term is 75 – 5 = 70 and the last term is 55 + 5 = 60.

14. D
The sequence is increasing by 6.

15. A
The sequence is increasing by 9.

16. D
The sequence is increasing and decreasing alternately. It increases by +5 and decreases by -7. The first term will thus be the second term 95 – 5 = 90 and the last term will be 91 – 7 = 84.

17. B
The difference between the terms starts from 12 and decreases by 2 i.e. 12, 10,8,6,4,2. The missing terms are 46 – 6 = 40 and 34 – 0 = 34.

18. D
Each term is being doubled or multiplied by 2 to get the next term. 3 x 2 = 6 and 12 x 2 = 24.

19. C
The sequence is increasing by 9.

20. C
The difference between the first two terms is 10. The difference between subsequent terms decreases by 1, i.e. 10, 9,8,7,6. Answer is 37 + 6 = 43.

Problem Solving

1. A
The price of 12 shirts with profit is 8% = 0.92 X 336 = $309.12 The purchase price of each shirt = 309.12/12 = $25.76

2. D
To find the total turnout in all three polling stations, we need to proportion the number of voters to the number of all registered voters.
Number of total voters = 945 + 860 + 1210 = 3015

Number of total registered voters = 1270 + 1050 + 1440 = 3760

Percentage turnout over all three polling stations = 3015 * 100/3760 = 80.19%

Checking the answers, we round 80.19 to the nearest whole number: 80%

3. B
Assume the total numbers of employees is x. The total salary of all employees will be 125x. The total salary of the managers = 10 X 300 = $3000. The number of employees = X - 10, so the total salary of employees will be 100 X (X-10). The equation becomes 100(X - 10) + 3000 = 125X. x = 40.

4. C
The number of remaining questions is 40 - 28 = 12
The time remaining is 30 - 25 = 5 minutes = 5 X 60 = 300 seconds. So the time remaining for each question is 300/12 = 25 seconds.

5. B
Total expense is $2000 and we are informed that $5 is spent per meter. Combining these two information, we know that the total length of the fence is 2000/5 = 400 meters.

The fence is built around a square-shaped field. If one side of the square is "a," the perimeter of the square is "4a." Here, the perimeter is equal to 400 meters. So,

400 = 4a

100 = a → this means that one side of the square is equal to 100 meters.

6. B
If 72 students are present, then 83 - 72 = 11 students are absent. To calculate the percent, the equation will be,

11/83 = x/100
83x = 1100
x = 1100/83
x = 13.25   rounding off - 13% of the students are absent.

7. C
Initial cost was $220. New cost = 220 + (45% of 220), 45% of 220, 45/100 x 220 = 99, therefore new price is 220 + 99 = $319

8. D
Let old salary = X, therefore $150 = x + 0.30x, 150 = 1x + 0.30x, 150 = 1.30x, x = 150/1.30 = 115.4

9. B
Flat Screen TVs are the third best-selling product.
10. B
The two products that are closest in the number of sales, are Flat Screen TVs and Radar Detectors.

11. B
Actual cost = X, therefore, 545 = x + 0.15x, 545 = 1x + 0.15x, 545 = 1.15x, x = 545/1.15 = 473.9

12. C
Initial cost was $220. New cost = 200 + 45% of 200, 45% of 200, 45/100 x 220 = 99, therefore new price is 220 + 99 = $319

13. D
First convert the unit of measurements to be the same. Since 1000 g = 1 kg, 10 kg = 10 x 1000 = 10,000 + 550 g = 10,550 g. Divide 10,550 among 5 = 10550/5 = 2110 = 2 kg 110 g

14. C
Each round trip will be 8 blocks, so in 5 days, he will drive 5 X 8 = 40 blocks.

15. D
The equation will be, X/2 - 250 = 3X/7
X = $3,500.

Conclusion

Congratulations! You have made it this far because you have applied yourself diligently to practicing for the exam and no doubt improved your potential score considerably! Getting into a good school is a huge step in a journey that might be challenging at times but will be many times more rewarding and fulfilling. That is why being prepared is so important.

Study then Practice and then Succeed!

Good Luck!

Register for Free Updates and More Practice Test Questions

Register your purchase at
https://www.test-preparation.ca/register/

for updates, free test tips and more practice test questions.

https://www.facebook.com/CompleteTestPreparation/

https://www.youtube.com/user/MrTestPreparation

Online Resources

How to Prepare for a Test - The Ultimate Guide

https://www.test-preparation.ca/prepare-test/

Learning Styles - The Complete Guide

https://www.test-preparation.ca/learning-style/

Test Anxiety Secrets!

https://www.test-preparation.ca/test-anxiety/

Time Management on a Test

https://www.test-preparation.ca/time-management/

Flash Cards - The Complete Guide

https://www.test-preparation.ca/flash-cards/

Test Preparation Video Series

https://www.test-preparation.ca/test-video/

How to Memorize - The Complete Guide

https://www.test-preparation.ca/memorize/

Online Library of Student Tips and Strategies

https://www.test-preparation.ca/students-say/

www.ingramcontent.com/pod-product-compliance
Lightning Source LLC
LaVergne TN
LVHW020346260326
834688LV00045B/1559